# 3-D SPACE

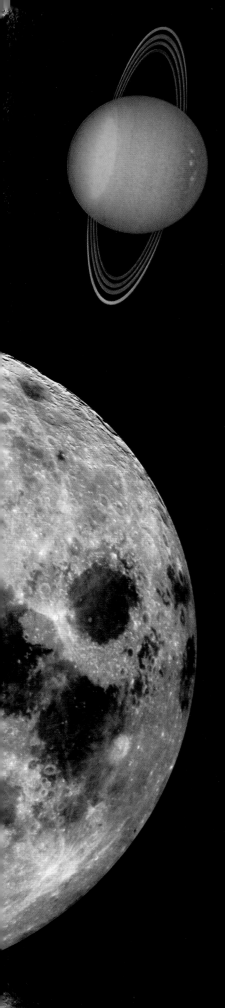

LONDON, NEW YORK,
MELBOURNE, MUNICH, AND
DELHI

**DK LONDON**
**Senior Art Editor** Jim Green
**Project Editor** Steven Carton
**Augmented Reality Development** Steven Carton
**Managing Editor** Linda Esposito
**Managing Art Editor** Diane Peyton Jones
**Category Publisher** Laura Buller

**Publishing Director** Jonathan Metcalf
**Associate Publishing Director** Liz Wheeler
**Art Director** Phil Ormerod

**Production Controller** Angela Graef
**Production Editor** Joanna Byrne
**DK Picture Library** Emma Shepherd, Rose Horridge
**Picture Research** Sean Hunter
**Design Development Manager** Sophia M. Tampakopoulos
**Jacket Editor** Manisha Majithia
**Jacket Designer** Laura Brim

**3-D Digital Artist** Arran Lewis

**For Pure Digital:**
**Director and Animation** Rob Cook
**Director and Programming** Paul Hetherington

**DK DELHI**
**Managing Art Editor** Arunesh Talapatra
**Senior Art Editor** Sudakshina Basu
**Art Editors** Shriya Parameswaran, Pallavi Narain

**Deputy Managing Editor** Pakshalika Jayaprakash
**Senior Editor** Garima Sharma
**Editor** Roma Malik

**Production Manager** Pankaj Sharma
**DTP Manager** Balwant Singh
**Senior DTP Designer** Dheeraj Arora
**DTP Designers** Nand Kishor Acharya, Tanveer Zaidi

AUGMENTED BY
TOTAL IMMERSION

First published in the United States in 2012
by DK Publishing
375 Hudson Street
New York, New York 10014

A catalog record for this book
is available from the Library of Congress.

ISBN 978-0-7566-9019-9

Hi-res workflow proofed by MDP, UK
Printed and bound in China by Hung Hing

Discover more at
**www.dk.com**

# 3-D
# SPACE

Written by
**Carole Stott**

# Contents

 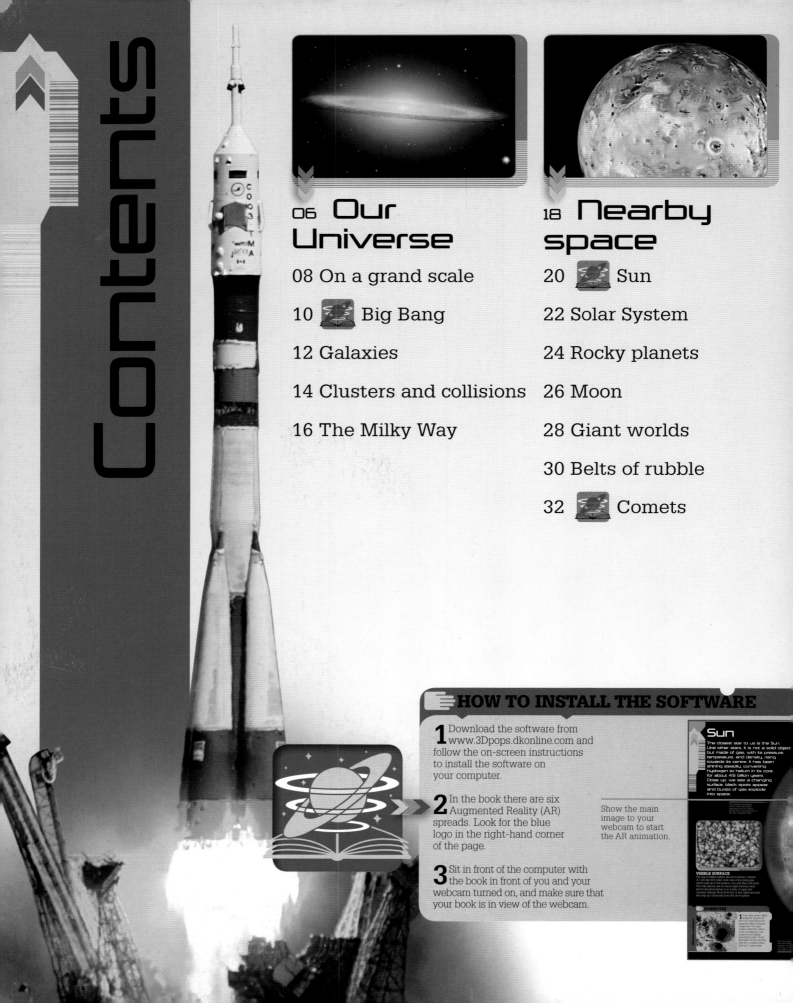
## HOW TO INSTALL THE SOFTWARE

**1** Download the software from www.3Dpops.dkonline.com and follow the on-screen instructions to install the software on your computer.

**2** In the book there are six Augmented Reality (AR) spreads. Look for the blue logo in the right-hand corner of the page.

**3** Sit in front of the computer with the book in front of you and your webcam turned on, and make sure that your book is in view of the webcam.

### Sun

The closest star to us is the Sun. Like other stars, it is not a solid object but made of gas, with its pressure, temperature, and density, rising towards its centre. It has been shining steadily, converting hydrogen to helium in its core, for about 4.6 billion years. Close up, we see a changing surface, black spots appear and bursts of gas explode into space.

Show the main image to your webcam to start the AR animation.

**VISIBLE SURFACE**

The Sun's visible surface, the photosphere, consists of 1,000 kilometre (620 mile) wide cells of hot rising gas, which rise up to the surface, cool, and then sink back. The cells are too small for amateur instruments to detect, and so the photosphere is in a state of rapid and constant change. Short-lived jets of gas called spicules also leap up continually from the photosphere.

**SUNSPOTS**

**1** Dark spots, some appear against the Sun's surface are called sunspots. The dark centre, called the umbra, is the coolest part. Around it is a lighter region, the penumbra. Sunspots can be seen crossing the Sun's surface as it rotates, and often in pairs or multiple forms.

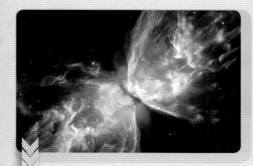

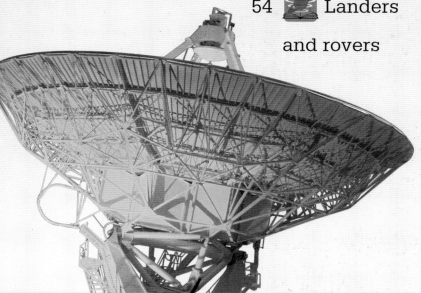

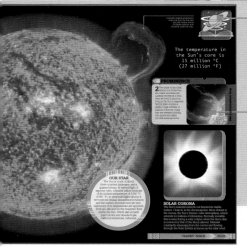

AR logo is in the right-hand corner of the AR spread.

Place your hand over each trigger box in turn to control the animation.

**4** Show the central image on the open page to the webcam and the AR animation will jump to life from the pages of your book and appear on your computer screen.

**5** To see the next part of the animation, place your hand over one of the trigger boxes. Each trigger box is labeled with a hand symbol to show that it is a trigger box, and the boxes are numbered in the order that they should be covered.

### Minimum system requirements

**Windows PC**
Windows XP with DirectX 9.0c
(or Windows XP SP2), Windows Vista Intel P4
2.4 GHz or Amd equivalent
1 Gb RAM
Supports most graphics cards (Nvidia, ATI, Chipset Intel) except Via chipset

**Macintosh**
Mac OS 10.4, 10.5, 10.6
Intel Dual Core (or Core 2 duo) 2.4Ghz
1 Gb RAM
Supports graphics cards Nvidia, ATI
(Macs based on Power PC processor are not supported)

# Our Universe

The Sombrero Galaxy
in infrared light

Humans live on a
blue, rocky ball called
planet Earth. It is big and
important to us, but tiny and
insignificant compared to the other
objects that make up the Universe. Earth
exists within the Milky Way Galaxy, a vast
grouping of billions of stars. Beyond are
billions more galaxies, of different kinds
and shapes. None of them has existed
forever and all share a common
origin—an event called the Big Bang
that created the Universe itself
almost 14 billion years ago.

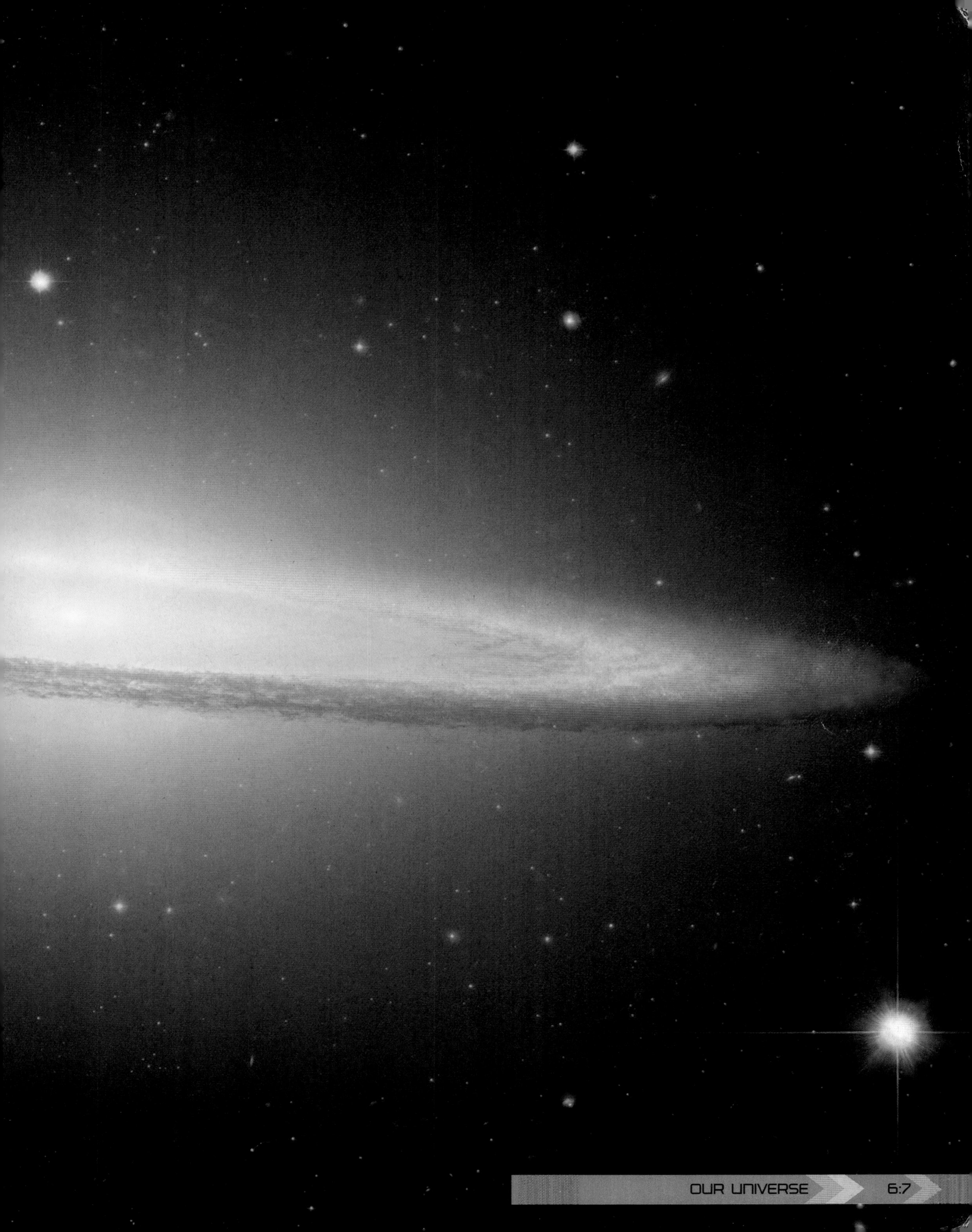

# On a grand scale

All that exists, including everything we know about, as well as everything undiscovered, makes up the Universe. Looking out from Earth, we can see much of the Universe. Nearby are other planets as well as the Sun, our closest star. In all directions around us are other stars, which together make up the Milky Way Galaxy. Beyond the limits of our own galaxy are billions of other galaxies revealed to us by telescopes, on Earth and in space, that have helped us to explore the Universe.

## THE UNIVERSE

Whichever direction and however deep we look, the Universe looks much the same. This typical view (right) is of a tiny patch of Earth's sky, looking through billions of light-years into distant space. Most of these objects are galaxies, some of the 125 billion that populate the Universe. Those that appear largest are the closest. The bright objects with starlike points are foreground stars within the Milky Way Galaxy.

## EVOLVING UNIVERSE

The Universe has been changing ever since it came into being 13.7 billion years ago. Throughout its history it has been made of the same amount of material but this has changed in form, and the Universe itself has grown in size. Today's Universe continues to expand and evolve. For instance, stars are being born within galaxies all the time. The closest star-forming region to us is NGC 3603 (right), which is continually producing stars from gas and dust. At its center is a cluster of thousands of young stars.

## LOCAL SPACE

Earth belongs to a tiny region of the Universe known as the Solar System. The system consists of the Sun and a family of objects traveling around it. Ours is just one of the system's eight planets, and the only place in the Universe known to have life. The Solar System is the only part of space that we have sent unmanned spacecraft to explore, and humans have only been as far as our nearest space neighbor, the Moon.

The scale starts at Earth's center. Its figures are in mathematical shorthand: $10^6$ means one followed by six zeros.

The divisions are not even. Each additional division is a tenfold increase on the previous one.

The Sun is an average of 93 million miles (149 million km) away from Earth.

The distance to the middle of the Kuiper Belt, a ring of ice and rock objects orbiting the Sun.

| 0 miles (0 km) | 6,200 miles (10,000 km) | 620,000 miles ($10^6$ km) | 62 million miles ($10^8$ km) | 6.2 billion miles ($10^{10}$ km) |

## LOOKING AT THE UNIVERSE

Astronomers study the Universe by collecting light and other forms of energy from space objects. Through analysis of this data, and by applying the laws of science to it, they make discoveries that add to our knowledge. Their fundamental tool for collecting the information is the telescope, and the most powerful of these are in space or based on mountaintop sites where they get the best possible view. These four telescope domes are part of the European Southern Observatory, high on Paranal Mountain in Chile.

## MISSING UNIVERSE

Stars, galaxies, and the like are made from atoms. But when added up, they only account for a small part of the total Universe. The majority consists of dark matter and dark energy. The unknown material, dark matter, doesn't emit energy and cannot be detected directly. We know it exists because it affects objects we can see. Dark energy, which speeds up the rate of expansion of the Universe, is even more mysterious.

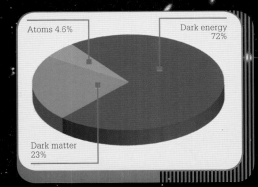

Atoms 4.6%

Dark energy 72%

Dark matter 23%

## LIGHT-YEAR

Distances are so vast in the Universe that the measuring units we use on Earth are inadequate. A unit called the light-year (ly) not only measures distances outside the Solar System but the size of the Universe's largest objects, such as galaxies. One light-year is the distance that light travels in a year—this is 5.88 trillion miles (9.46 trillion kilometers). The scale below measures out to the edge of the visible Universe.

The closest star to Earth after the Sun is Proxima Centauri, which is 4.2 light-years away.

At 1,000 light-years from Earth, 90 percent of all stars seen by eye alone are within this distance.

$6.2 \times 10^{13}$ miles ($10^{14}$ km)     $6.2 \times 10^{15}$ miles ($10^{16}$ km)     $6.2 \times 10^{17}$ miles ($10^{18}$ km)     $6.2 \times 10^{19}$ miles ($10^{20}$ km)     $6.2 \times 10^{21}$ miles ($10^{22}$ km)

# Big Bang

The Universe started in an explosive event called the Big Bang about 13.7 billion years ago. It was not only the start of all the material that makes up the galaxies, stars, and planets, but of energy, gravity, and space and time, too. Today's Universe is very different from the one way back then. Although made up of the same amount of material and energy, the Universe has been continuously changing. It has been cooling and expanding since the start, and its form has altered to produce the Universe of galaxies that exists today.

Over millions of years hydrogen and helium clumped together into vast clouds. These broke into fragments to form stars and created the first galaxies.

## EXPLOSIVE START

See the Universe begin

**1** At the beginning, the Universe was very small and dense, and made only of energy. It was also super hot, about 1,800 trillion trillion °F (1,000 trillion trillion °C). Within a second, the Universe exploded in size, and its energy particles turned into matter, which has changed over time.

TIME ⟶

| 1 MINUTE | 300,000 YEARS | 200 MILLION YEARS | 1 BILLION YEARS |

BIG BANG

## DYING HEAT

Some galaxies are so distant from Earth that their light takes billions of years to reach us. This means we see them as they were billions of years ago. We are unable to look all the way back to the Big Bang, but we have detected its dying heat. Known as cosmic microwave background radiation, maps of the heat (left) show that the young Universe's material was not evenly distributed. Hotter, more densely packed regions (yellow) gave birth to galaxies.

The Universe becomes transparent once atoms of hydrogen and helium form. These go on to produce all the elements in today's Universe.

## EARLY EARTH

Along with everything else in the Universe, Earth has changed greatly since its beginnings. Formed from leftover material that made the Sun, the young Earth was a red-hot semimolten ball of rock and metal. As it cooled, it solidified from the surface down. Volcanoes spewed out dust, gas, and rock (right). Eventually, steam in the atmosphere cooled to produce rain, and this collected to form Earth's oceans, which is where the first signs of life appeared.

## THE STORY OF THE UNIVERSE

For the first 300,000 years or so, the Universe was like a hot, foggy soup of tiny particles of matter. These formed the first atoms, hydrogen and helium, which over tens of millions of years made the first stars and galaxies. By the time it was a billion years old, the Universe was full of dwarf galaxies. These collided and merged over time to form the present-day galaxies.

Massive galaxies grow from the first dwarf galaxies.

3 BILLION YEARS     5 BILLION YEARS     7 BILLION YEARS     9 BILLION YEARS

Processes both inside stars, and during the death of massive stars, produce new elements such as carbon and oxygen.

## OUR PLACE IN THE UNIVERSE

**2** The disk-shaped Milky Way Galaxy formed at the same time as the Universe's other galaxies. An unremarkable star we now call the Sun formed inside this galaxy about 4.6 billion years ago. Material remaining from the star-making process produced planets, including Earth.

**Zoom across the Universe to Earth**

# Galaxies

Enormous collections of stars, gas, dust, and dark matter bound together by gravity are called galaxies. They range in size from dwarf galaxies only a few thousand light-years across to the biggest, about 300,000 light-years wide. Even the smallest galaxies contain about 10 million stars, and the largest have as many as a trillion. Galaxies are classed according to their shape: elliptical, spiral, barred-spiral, and irregular.

## ELLIPTICAL

Elliptical galaxies are collections of generally older stars. These galaxies have little gas and dust, and limited star-formation. They come in a range of ball shapes, from nearly spherical to flattened oval. Compared to other galaxies, they are smooth, almost featureless structures. Most of the stars in NGC 4150 (right) are around 10 billion years old but this elliptical also contains some younger stars. A merger with a dwarf galaxy about one billion years ago provided the gas and triggered star birth in the center.

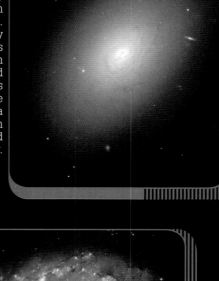

## BARRED-SPIRAL

Galaxies such as NGC 1672 (above) have many of the same qualities as spiral galaxies. In particular, they are disk-shaped and have spiral arms. But the arms of these galaxies wind out from a distinct bar of stars rather than a rounded bulge. This means they are classed as barred-spirals. Uniquely, they channel gas and dust from the disk in toward the galaxy's nucleus. In this way they fuel the central black hole, and also star formation in the bar.

## STAR ISLANDS

The galaxies are huge and widely separated objects, like colossal star islands strewn through space. This galaxy is NGC 2841, a spiral galaxy about 150,000 light-years across and 46 million light-years away. It is classed as a spiral galaxy because it consists of a star-packed central bulge surrounded by a flat disk of stars, gas, and dust. Within the disk are arms of stars that spiral out from the central bulge.

## IRREGULAR

Some galaxies have no regular shape or form and are classed as irregular. They are relatively small and contain much gas and dust, as well as a high proportion of young and newly formed stars. Hundreds of massive young blue stars are glowing brightly in the center of NGC 4214 (left). They are encircled by a huge bubble carved out in the surrounding gas by ultraviolet energy and winds emitted by the stars. Each star is 10,000 times brighter than the Sun, with wind speeding away at thousands of miles per second.

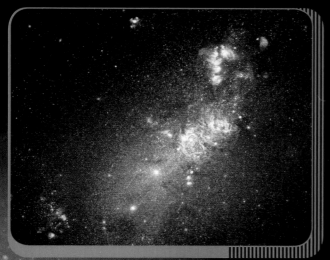

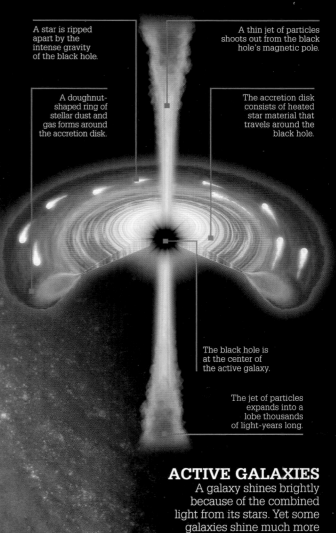

A star is ripped apart by the intense gravity of the black hole.

A thin jet of particles shoots out from the black hole's magnetic pole.

A doughnut-shaped ring of stellar dust and gas forms around the accretion disk.

The accretion disk consists of heated star material that travels around the black hole.

The black hole is at the center of the active galaxy.

The jet of particles expands into a lobe thousands of light-years long.

## ACTIVE GALAXIES

A galaxy shines brightly because of the combined light from its stars. Yet some galaxies shine much more brightly than expected. Their extra brilliance comes from activity in their centers, around a black hole, and for this reason they are known as active galaxies. Star material orbits around the galaxy's black hole before falling in. It forms a disklike structure called the accretion disk that heats up and radiates intense energy. Some material also jets out from either side of the hole.

# Clusters and collisions

Galaxies first formed billions of years ago. Since then, they have evolved through collisions and mergers, changing in shape, size, and mass. Individual galaxies also change as stars form, live, and die within them. Today, galaxies are not scattered randomly across the Universe but exist in clusters. These in turn form larger groupings called superclusters, which are the largest structures in the Universe. The huge empty voids that separate them give the Universe a spongelike appearance.

## CLUSTERED TOGETHER

A galaxy cluster can contain as many as a few thousand galaxies. The Coma Cluster (above) contains at least one thousand, is roughly spherical in shape, and about 20 million light-years across. This view is one-third of the way out from the cluster's center, and includes elliptical galaxies as well as a spiral galaxy (upper left). Huge expanses of space separate one galaxy cluster from another. As the Universe expands, the clusters get farther apart.

## GALACTIC COLLISIONS

Galaxies meet and interact over hundreds of millions of years. Stars within the galaxies don't usually collide but huge clouds of gas within the galaxies do, and these collisions initiate star birth. The Antennae Galaxies (right) are two interacting spiral galaxies. A brown gas-and-dust cloud links the bright cores of the original galaxies; glowing hydrogen gas appears pink and new star-forming regions are blue.

## LOCAL GROUP

Our Milky Way Galaxy belongs to a small cluster called the Local Group, which consists of more than 40 galaxies. The Milky Way and the Andromeda Galaxy (right) are the two largest and the dominant members. About ten of the Local Group's smaller galaxies orbit the Andromeda. One of them, the dwarf elliptical galaxy M110, is visible at lower right. Andromeda is getting closer to the Milky Way by about 186 miles (300 km) every second. The two may collide in about 4 billion years time.

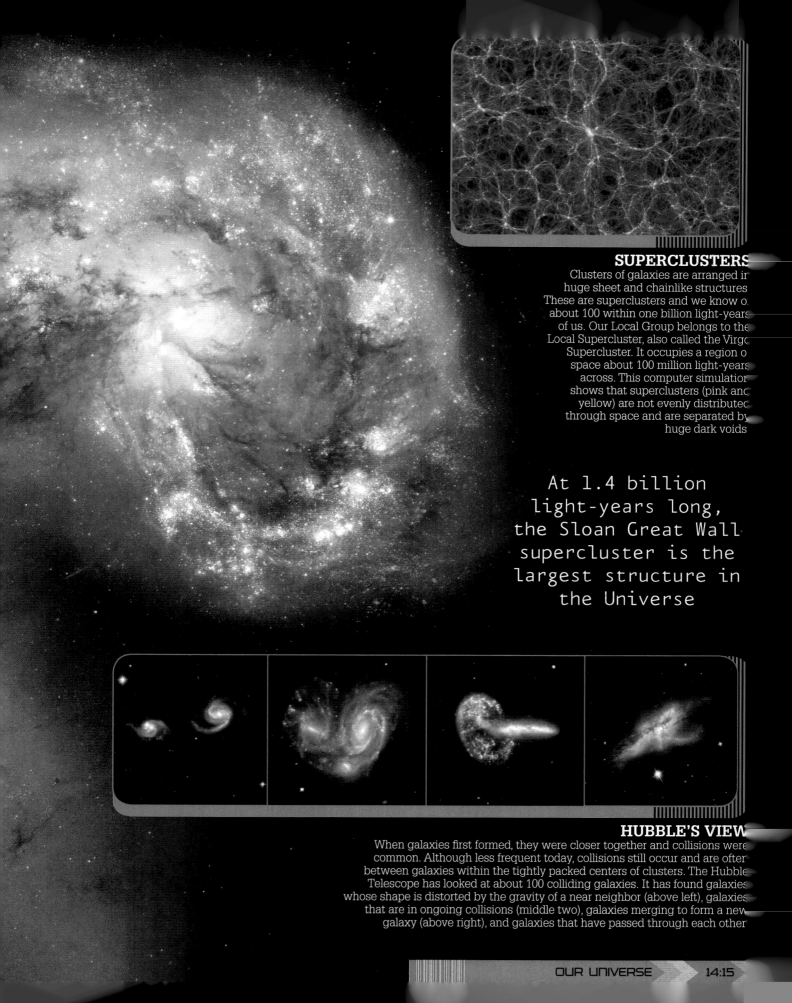

## SUPERCLUSTERS

Clusters of galaxies are arranged in huge sheet and chainlike structures. These are superclusters and we know of about 100 within one billion light-years of us. Our Local Group belongs to the Local Supercluster, also called the Virgo Supercluster. It occupies a region of space about 100 million light-years across. This computer simulation shows that superclusters (pink and yellow) are not evenly distributed through space and are separated by huge dark voids

At 1.4 billion
light-years long,
the Sloan Great Wall
supercluster is the
largest structure in
the Universe

## HUBBLE'S VIEW

When galaxies first formed, they were closer together and collisions were common. Although less frequent today, collisions still occur and are often between galaxies within the tightly packed centers of clusters. The Hubble Telescope has looked at about 100 colliding galaxies. It has found galaxies whose shape is distorted by the gravity of a near neighbor (above left), galaxies that are in ongoing collisions (middle two), galaxies merging to form a new galaxy (above right), and galaxies that have passed through each other

# The Milky Way

The Milky Way Galaxy is an enormous disk-shaped collection of stars, gas, and dust. Our local star, the Sun, is just one of the 400 billion or so stars within the galaxy. The Milky Way is classed as a barred spiral galaxy since the central region of its disk is elongated into a bar shape, and arms wind out from either end of it. The Sun and its system of planets, including Earth and the Moon, are in one of the spiral arms.

The yellow color of the central bulge comes from its red and yellow stars.

## HOME GALAXY

If we could travel outside the Milky Way, we would see that it is not flat like a computer disk, but that it has a central bulge. In this bulge are old, red and yellow stars. The arms are made of both young and more mature stars, such as the Sun. From one side of the disk to the other is 100,000 light-years. A spherical halo of more than 180 collections of old stars, called globular clusters, completely surrounds the disk.

The Perseus Arm is one of the galaxy's two distinct, main arms.

The Norma Arm is one of two minor arms rich in gas and star-forming regions.

The Scutum-Centaurus Arm winds out of the opposite end of the central bar to the other main arm, Perseus.

The Sagittarius Arm is one of two minor arms positioned between the major arms.

## SPIRAL ARMS

The Milky Way's disk has two main spiral arms, two minor ones, and a partial arm that contains the Sun. Although not immediately visible, there are also young and mature stars between the arms. They are not obvious because the many young stars in the arms are particularly bright and outshine them. The stars in the disk follow their own orbits around the galaxy's center. The Sun takes 220 million years to go around once.

The Sun is within the Orion Arm, about 27,000 light-years from the galaxy's center.

## VIEW FROM INSIDE

All the stars that we see scattered across Earth's sky belong to the Milky Way Galaxy. When we see these stars we are looking through the depth of the galaxy's disk. But when we look along the plane of the galaxy's disk we see many more stars. These appear in the sky as a long trail of stars wrapped around Earth (left). This milky path of light, which contains bands of dust and dark gas too, is also called the Milky Way.

The disk, here seen edge on, is about 4,000 light-years deep.

**The Sun travels around the Milky Way's center at about 500,000 mph (800,000 kph)**

## MILKY LIGHT

The ancient Greeks observed the path of the Milky Way in Earth's sky and explained it as milk spilled by the goddess Hera when feeding baby Heracles (below). They described the path as *galaxias*, meaning "milky," and this became our word galaxy. The Romans called it *Via Lactea* ("milky road" in Latin). Centuries later, in 1610, astronomer Galileo Galilei was the first to use a telescope to study the path and he discovered it is made of stars.

The black hole Sagittarius A* is within this bright region.

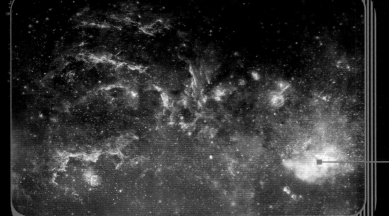

## HEART OF THE GALAXY

In the Milky Way's heart is a supermassive black hole called Sagittarius A*. It is millions of miles across and thought to be as massive as about four million Suns. It probably formed when the Milky Way was young and a huge gas cloud collapsed in on itself. In this colorful view, yellow areas are where stars are being born, red is glowing dust clouds, and blue is gas heated to millions of degrees.

# Nearby space

Earth and its close neighbor, the Moon, belong to a space family called the Solar System. They exist together in a tiny corner of the Milky Way Galaxy. Central to the system is the Sun, a massive luminous ball of gas. The other family members are a mixed bunch of objects, which orbit around it. There are rocky worlds covered in craters and volcanoes, giant planets with surfaces of swirling gas, and comets that grow spectacularly long tails.

Io, Jupiter's third largest moon and the most volcanic place in the Solar System

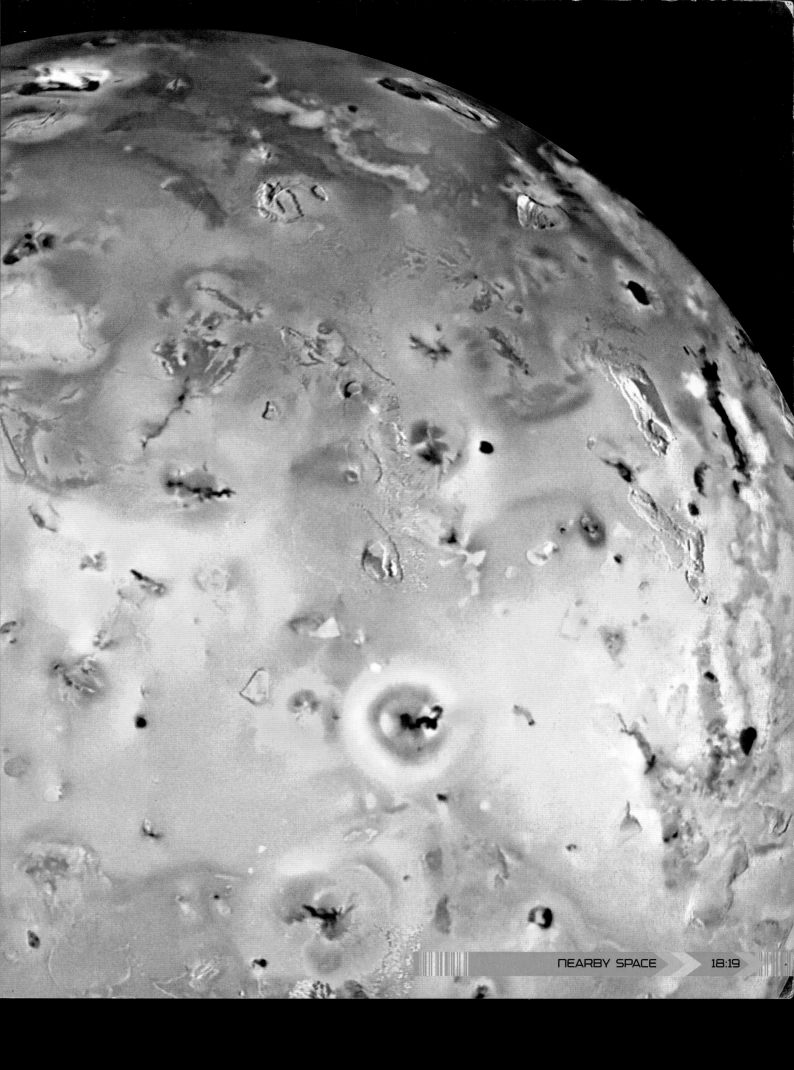

# Sun

The closest star to us is the Sun. Like other stars, it is not a solid object but made of gas, with its pressure, temperature, and density rising towards its center. It has been shining steadily, converting hydrogen to helium in its core, for about 4.6 billion years. Close up, we see a changing surface, as black spots appear and bursts of gas explode into space.

The hottest parts appear almost white and denote particularly active regions produced by concentrations in the Sun's magnetic field.

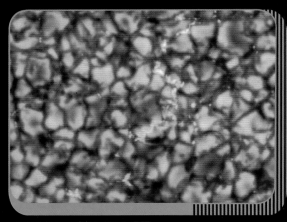

## VISIBLE SURFACE

The Sun's visible surface, the photosphere, consists of 620-mile (1,000-km) wide cells of hot rising gas, which rush up to the surface, cool, and then sink back. The cells (above) last for about eight minutes each, and thus the photosphere is in a state of rapid and constant change. Short-lived jets of gas called spicules also leap up continually from the photosphere.

## SUNSPOTS

Observe a sunspot

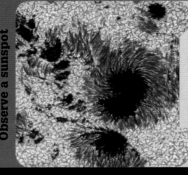

**1** Cool, dark areas, called sunspots, appear on the Sun's face where its magnetic field interrupts rising heat. The dark center, called the umbra, is the coolest part. It is ringed by the lighter penumbra region. Each spot lasts for two months, and their number varies over an 11-year cycle.

The chromosphere— the inner atmosphere— extends out about 1,550 miles (2,500 km) from the visible surface.

A handle-shaped prominence loops out from the Sun and into the corona. About 20 Earths side-by-side would fit under the loop.

The temperature in the Sun's core is 27 million °F (15 million °C)

## PROMINENCE

**2** The loops or arcs that extend out of the Sun are called prominences. Lasting months at a time, they are held in place as long as the Sun's magnetic field in their vicinity is stable. Huge bubbles of billions of tons of gas that are released directly into space are called coronal mass ejections.

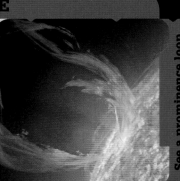

*See a prominence loop*

### OUR STAR
The Sun is made of about three-quarters hydrogen, and a quarter helium. In natural light, it appears calm, colored yellow because of its surface temperature of 9,900°F (5,500°C). In ultraviolet light (above) it becomes an orange incandescent furnace, and the surface structure and the nonuniformity of its temperature are apparent. Both are affected by the magnetic field inside the Sun, which also propels giant clouds and sheets of gas, called prominences, outward.

### SOLAR CORONA
The Sun's material extends out beyond its visible surface. Close in is the chromosphere. More distant is the corona, the Sun's thinner, outer atmosphere, which extends for millions of miles. Normally invisible, this is seen during a solar eclipse, when the Sun's disk is covered by that of the Moon (above). Material constantly streaming from the corona and flowing through the Solar System is known as the solar wind.

# Solar System

The Sun and the family of objects orbiting around it is known as the Solar System. After the Sun, the major family members are the eight planets, more than 160 moons that orbit the planets, and five dwarf planets. Minor members are a lot smaller but much more numerous. They include billions of asteroids, Kuiper Belt objects, and comets. All the Solar System objects formed about 4.6 billion years ago and they have been together ever since.

1. The center of the cloud became dense and heated up as gravity pulled material in.

2. A disk of gas, dust, and ice particles that bumped and joined together surrounded the young Sun.

3. Rocky planets formed close to the Sun. In the cooler outer disk, rocky bodies attracted gas and formed giant planets.

## FAMILY HISTORY

The Solar System formed from a slowly spinning cloud of gas and dust called the solar nebula. Gravity pulled material in toward the cloud's center, which made the cloud spin faster. The center became denser, heated up, and eventually formed the Sun. Unused material formed a spinning disk around the young star. Over millions of years, the material in the disk bumped and joined together into larger and larger pieces, eventually forming the planets.

Earth is the only Solar System body known to have life and liquid water on its surface.

One complete circuit of the Sun is called an orbit. Planets orbit counterclockwise when viewed from above the Sun's North Pole.

Massive Jupiter is the innermost of the giant planets. It has the highest amount of moons of any planet, with 63.

## SUN'S FAMILY

Closest to the Sun are the four rock-and-metal planets: Mercury, Venus, Earth, and Mars. More distant are four larger planets, the giant worlds of Jupiter, Saturn, Uranus, and Neptune, made mainly from gas and liquid. A belt of asteroids lies between the two groups. The gravity of the Sun holds all its family members in orbit around it. The objects spin on their axes as they orbit, which creates night and day on the planets.

The Asteroid Belt consists of billions of asteroids: rock and metal objects following their own orbits.

The Sun

Grey Mercury is the smallest planet and closest to the Sun. It completes one orbit in just 88 days.

Uranus is twice as far from the Sun as Saturn, and takes 84 years for one orbit.

SUN
MERCURY
VENUS
EARTH
MARS
JUPITER
SATURN

## BEYOND NEPTUNE

A belt of ice and rock bodies called the Kuiper Belt stretches for billions of miles beyond Neptune. The outer edge of the belt merges into a vast sphere made up of more than a trillion comets called the Oort Cloud. The comets follow individual elongated orbits around the Sun in every direction. The far edge of the Oort Cloud is nearly halfway to the nearest stars and marks the distant boundary of the Solar System.

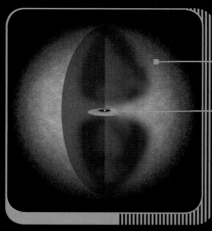

Oort Cloud of comets

Kuiper Belt of ice and rock objects

## OTHER MEMBERS

Six of the eight planets have moons orbiting around them, sharing more than 160 moons between them. They are made mainly of rock such as Phobos and Io, or rock and ice, like Europa. The largest, Ganymede, is bigger than Mercury. Pluto, about half the size of Mercury, was once the ninth Solar System planet, but was reclassified as a dwarf planet in 2006.

Phobos

Pluto

Europa

Io

Mars is about one-and-a-half times the distance of Earth from the Sun, making it a much colder world.

Saturn is the second largest planet. It takes 29.5 years to make one orbit of the Sun.

Neptune is so far out that it has completed just one orbit since its discovery.

Venus is the slowest-spinning planet. It turns once in 243 days, longer than its orbit of 225 days.

URANUS

NEPTUNE

## DISTANCES

Miles or kilometers are used to describe distances within the Solar System. For instance, Earth is 93 million miles (149 million km) from the Sun. Astronomers refer to this distance as one astronomical unit (1 au), and using it makes describing distances easier. For instance, Saturn is 9.5 au from the Sun. However, such figures give the average distance a planet is from the Sun. Distances differ because planets travel on elliptical orbits, which at times take them nearer and then farther away from the Sun.

1,550 MILES (2,500 KM)　　　1,860 MILES (3,000 KM)　　　2,200 MILES (3,500 KM)　　　2,500 MILES (4,000 KM)　　　2,800 MILES (4,500 KM)

# Rocky planets

Mercury, Venus, Earth, and Mars are the four closest planets to the Sun, and are commonly called the rocky planets even though they are partly made of metal. In spite of their similar makeup, the four are very different worlds. Mercury is heavily cratered; hot and gloomy Venus is covered in volcanic lava; Earth has liquid water and life; and much of red Mars is freezing-cold desert.

## RED PLANET

Sometimes called the red planet, Mars's coloring comes from its soil, which contains iron oxide (rust) and covers most of its surface. Just two vast regions, the planet's white caps at the north and south poles, stand out. Mars once had liquid water, as Earth does now, and it also spins on its axis in about 24 hours—but is only roughly half our planet's size. It features enormous volcanoes and the Valles Marineris, a huge system of canyons.

## CRATERED MERCURY

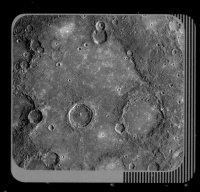

Mercury and the other three rocky planets were bombarded by asteroids more than 3.5 billion years ago. Bowl-shaped hollows called impact craters formed as asteroids hit the planets' surfaces. Most of Earth's craters and many on Venus and Mars have vanished due to geological activity and weather erosion, but millions of craters still cover Mercury's surface (left).

## HOT VENUS

Almost equal to Earth in size, Venus is a hostile world. Looking at it we see the top of a deep carbon-dioxide rich atmosphere that completely covers the planet. This gas layer, combined with the planet's proximity to the Sun, make it an oppressively hot and gloomy world under the clouds. The surface temperature is at an almost constant 867°F (464°C) both day and night.

## HOME PLANET

Earth is the largest of the four rocky planets. It also stands out because of the vast oceans of water that cover more than 70 percent of its surface and make it appear blue from space. Its rocky crust is broken into moving plates that rub against each other causing earthquakes, mountain formation, and volcanic eruptions. The land and oceans are home to billions of life forms, and Earth is the only place in the Universe where life is known to exist.

The volcano Olympus Mons built up from thousands of lava flows. This bird's eye view looks down at the caldera on its summit from which lava flowed.

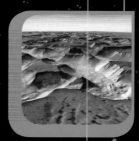

Noctis Labyrinthus, a huge region of canyons and troughs at one end of Valles Marineris, formed when unstable ground collapsed after the ice under it melted.

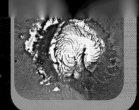

A permanent cap of water ice up to 1.2 miles (2 km) deep covers the north polar region. In the winter months, the 560-mile (900 km) wide cap is covered by carbon-dioxide snow.

Mars has two tiny moons, Phobos and Deimos, which were once asteroids

## VOLCANIC WORLDS

Volcanic activity has occurred on all four rocky planets. Its effect is most obvious on the present surfaces of Venus and Mars. Most of Venus is a low-lying plain covered in volcanic lava that erupted onto its surface hundreds of millions of years ago. The planet has hundreds of volcanoes, some of which may still be active. Maat Mons (right) is the highest, standing about 3 miles (5 km) above the surrounding land. The biggest volcanoes are on Mars. At 14 miles (22 km) tall, Olympus Mons is the tallest in the Solar System.

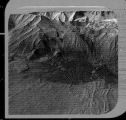

Valles Marineris extends about a quarter of the way around Mars. The canyon system formed when Mars's young surface pulled apart. This is Melas Chasma, a huge canyon in its center.

## INSIDE THE PLANETS

When the rocky planets were young, their material was molten. Since then, it has been cooling and settling into layers. Metals such as iron and nickel sank toward the center and the rocks, which are lighter, floated above. Today these layers are either wholly or partially solidified depending on their temperature and pressure. The smallest planet, Mercury, had the largest proportion of metal and this formed a huge metal core. The interiors of the two largest rock planets, Venus and Earth, are similar.

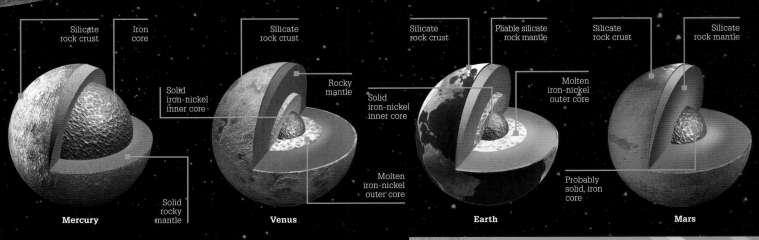

Silicate rock crust | Iron core

Solid iron-nickel inner core

Solid rocky mantle

**Mercury**

Silicate rock crust

Rocky mantle

Solid iron-nickel inner core

Molten iron-nickel outer core

**Venus**

Silicate rock crust | Pliable silicate rock mantle

Solid iron-nickel inner core

Molten iron-nickel outer core

**Earth**

Silicate rock crust | Silicate rock mantle

Probably solid, iron core

**Mars**

# Moon

Earth's closest space neighbor is the Moon. It has been orbiting around us ever since it formed as the result of an asteroid collision with Earth in the distant past. About a quarter of Earth's size, it appears larger than any other object in the night sky. From Earth, we only ever see one side of the Moon. We call this the near side and it appears to change shape over 29.5 days.

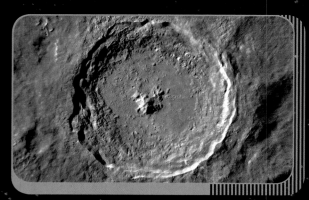

## CRATERED LANDSCAPE

Craters are found all over the Moon. As asteroids crashed into the lunar surface, the ground exploded outward and bowl-shaped hollows formed. The edges of the craters pushed up and became highlands. And in the center of the largest craters, such as 53-mile- (85-km-) wide Tycho Crater (above), the ground rebounded and created mountainous peaks.

## LUNAR SURFACE

The Moon is a dry ball of rock close enough to Earth for us to make out dark and light patches on its surface. The dark areas are huge craters with volcanic lava floors, and the brighter areas are higher land. The surface formed about 3.5 billion years ago and has changed very little. First, it was bombarded by asteroids and the craters formed. Then lava seeped through cracks in the Moon's crust and flooded the largest craters.

## ORIGIN OF THE MOON

**Asteroid hits Earth**
Most astronomers think the Moon formed when a Mars-sized asteroid gave the young Earth a glancing blow, ejecting rock, dust, and gas into space.

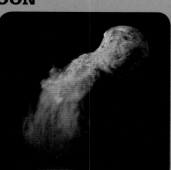

**Cloud of material**
Some of the material that broke away from Earth joined with material from the asteroid to form a hot cloud in orbit around Earth, which gradually cooled.

**Ring around Earth**
The cloud material eventually formed a doughnut-shaped ring around the planet. The pieces of material bumped and joined to form ever-larger pieces.

**Moon formed**
The pieces continued to bump and join, and cool. After a few tens of millions of years, one large body—the Moon (middle left)—was formed, and continued to orbit.

## MOON MOUNTAINS

Unlike Earth's mountains, which took shape as its plates pushed into each other, all of the Moon's mountains are in the center of craters or form crater rims. If it wasn't for cratering, the lunar surface would be smooth. The largest craters, known as mare, are edged by the longest mountain ranges. The Montes Apenninus (Apennine Mountains) form part of the rim of Mare Imbrium (above). The range is 373 miles (600 km) long and the highest peak is 3 miles (5 km)

Half of the near side is lit as the Moon starts the last quarter of the cycle.

A waning crescent is visible as the cycle is almost at its end.

The Moon has completed more than half its cycle and is waning (shrinking).

**7. Last quarter**

**8. Waning crescent**

**6. Waning gibbous**

The Moon is on the opposite side of Earth from the Sun, and we see a fully lit near side

**Moon's orbit**

**Earth**

**Sunlight**

**5. Full Moon**

The face of the new Moon is unlit, and cannot be seen clearly from Earth.

**1. New Moon**

A crescent-shaped slice of Moon waxes (grows) after the new Moon.

**2. Waxing crescent**

A quarter of the Moon's orbit has now been completed.

About three-quarters of the Moon's near side is sunlit. "Gibbous" means "lump-shaped."

**4. Waxing gibbous**

**3. First quarter**

## LUNAR PHASES

The Moon produces no light but shines by reflecting sunlight. Just like Earth, half of the Moon is always lit by the Sun, and the other half is dark (inner ring of Moons). The Moon's near side is sometimes fully lit by the Sun, sometimes partially lit, and at other times not at all (outer ring of Moons). The different-sized sunlit parts we see are the Moon's phases, and a full cycle of phases takes 29.5 days.

# Giant worlds

Jupiter, Saturn, Uranus, and Neptune are the most distant planets from the Sun and the largest in the Solar System. They are ice-cold ringed worlds made largely of gas and liquid. As we look at them, we see the tops of their thick and deep gas atmospheres. Jupiter and Saturn have been known since ancient times, but the other two were only discovered relatively recently.

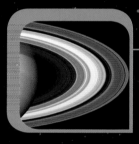

All rings are made of pieces that range up to room-sized boulders. Green indicates particles smaller than 2 in (5 cm). Purple indicates a lack of particles this small.

## LARGEST GIANT

Jupiter is the largest Solar System planet. It is so huge that 11 Earths could fit across its face. It is the most massive planet, made of 2.5 times the material of the other seven planets combined. Jupiter takes 12 years to complete one orbit, but one full rotation on its axis takes under 10 hours, faster than any other planet. Its rapid spin, along with strong winds and the Sun's heat, produce the colorful bands in its visible surface.

Oval, cloudlike structures are giant storms. This one, called the Great Red Spot, has been raging on Jupiter for more than 300 years and is the largest storm in the Solar System.

## BEAUTIFUL RINGS

A broad and complex system of rings distinguishes Saturn from the other giant worlds. The system looks solid from a distance, but consists of seven main rings made of hundreds of ringlets. These in turn are made from chunks of dirty water ice that follow their own orbits around the planet. High-altitude haze and Saturn's pale yellow color make it appear a calm world. But, like Jupiter, its atmosphere moves in bands around the planet, and ferocious storms rage.

## ON ITS SIDE

Twice as far from the Sun as Saturn, Uranus seems to roll around the Sun on its side. This is because the planet is tilted over by 98°, probably the result of a collision with a planet-sized body when Uranus was young. Its ring system and 27 moons circle its equator but, due to the tilt, appear to go around from top to bottom. To the eye, Uranus is a featureless pale blue world, but false color (left) highlights atmospheric layers and high clouds.

## BLUE NEPTUNE

Deep-blue Neptune is the smallest of the giant worlds, and the most distant of all Solar System planets. Its coloring, like Uranus's, is due to the methane in its atmosphere absorbing red light. About 2.8 billion miles (4.5 billion km) from the Sun, it takes 164.9 years to complete one orbit, longer than any other planet. At this great distance the Sun appears 900 times dimmer than on Earth, and Neptune's cloud-top temperature is an icy -330°F (-201°C).

Clumped together, the material in Saturn's rings would make a moon about 120 miles (193 km) across

### DISCOVERY

Until 1781, the Solar System was thought to have only six planets. These were Mercury, Venus, Earth, Mars, Jupiter, and Saturn, which had all been known of since humans first studied the sky. When English astronomer William Herschel (right) discovered Uranus in 1781, he thought at first he had found a comet, but soon realized his discovery. Later astronomers observing Uranus saw it wasn't moving along its orbit as expected, and predicted another planet was affecting it. In 1846, German Johann Galle discovered Neptune.

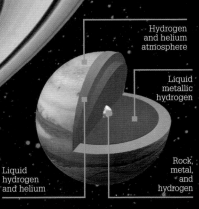

| Jupiter |
|---|

Hydrogen and helium atmosphere

Liquid metallic hydrogen

Liquid hydrogen and helium

Rock, metal, and hydrogen

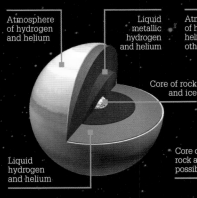

**Saturn**

Atmosphere of hydrogen and helium

Liquid metallic hydrogen and helium

Core of rock and ice

Liquid hydrogen and helium

Atmosphere of hydrogen, helium and other gases

Core of rock and possibly ice

**Uranus**

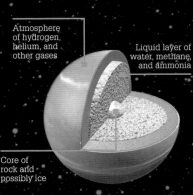

Liquid layer of water, methane, and ammonia

Atmosphere of hydrogen, helium, and other gases

Liquid layer of water, methane, and ammonia

Core of rock and possibly ice

**Neptune**

## INSIDE THE PLANETS

The atmospheres of all four giants are mainly hydrogen and helium gas. Underneath, Jupiter and Saturn are still mainly hydrogen and helium, but in different states. Uranus and Neptune are mainly water, methane, and ammonia. Moving toward the centers of these four planets, the material they are made of becomes increasingly tightly packed. Density, pressure, and temperature increase and affect the materials' physical states. At first they are liquidlike; deeper still they are like a liquid metal. In their centers are rocky cores.

# Belts of rubble

Two doughnut-shaped belts of objects encircle the Sun. These are the Asteroid Belt and the Kuiper Belt, and both are made of material left over from when the planets formed. Asteroids are made of rock and metal, and the Asteroid Belt is the remains of a planet that failed to form between Mars and Jupiter. The Kuiper Belt objects are made of ice and rock and lie beyond the most distant planet, Neptune.

## THE ASTEROID BELT

Billions of asteroids make up the Asteroid Belt (also called the Main Belt). Most are irregular in shape and less than 18.6 miles (30 km) across, and stay in the belt, but Jupiter's gravity can force asteroids out and into orbits that bring them into the inner Solar System. Those with paths that cross or approach Earth's orbit are called near-Earth asteroids. More than 215,000 asteroids have been identified and 15,000 have been given names.

Gaspra is 11.2 miles (18 km) long and orbits the Sun every 3.3 years within the Asteroid Belt. It was the first asteroid to be seen close-up, when the Galileo craft flew by in 1991.

Toutatis, just 2.8 miles (4.5 km) long, has been forced out of the belt by Jupiter's gravity. Its four-year orbit takes it within Earth's orbit and far beyond that of Mars.

Ceres was the first asteroid to be discovered, in 1901. It is the largest asteroid, and became a dwarf planet in 2006.

More than 90 percent of all asteroids are in the Asteroid Belt. Each asteroid follows its own path around the Sun.

Neptune's orbit

Uranus's orbit

The Kuiper Belt

Pluto's orbit

Sun

## KUIPER BELT

Starting about 3.7 billion miles (6 billion km) from the Sun, the Kuiper Belt is close to Neptune's orbit, and stretches away the same distance again. It was predicted to exist in the mid-20th century, but the first Kuiper Belt object was only discovered in 1992. New ones are discovered regularly. More than 1,000 are now known and many more are thought to exist.

Trojan asteroids travel around the Sun along a similar path to Jupiter. This group follows Jupiter, and the other (above right) leads the planet.

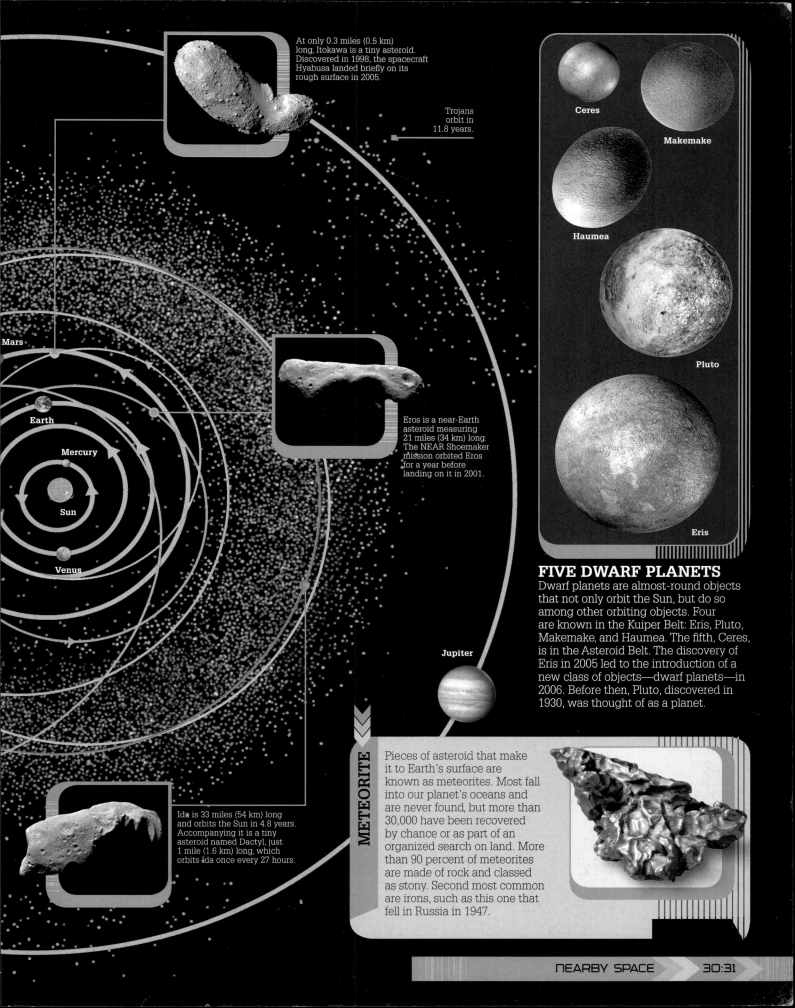

At only 0.3 miles (0.5 km) long, Itokawa is a tiny asteroid. Discovered in 1998, the spacecraft Hyabusa landed briefly on its rough surface in 2005.

Trojans orbit in 11.8 years.

Mars

Earth

Mercury

Sun

Venus

Eros is a near-Earth asteroid measuring 21 miles (34 km) long. The NEAR Shoemaker mission orbited Eros for a year before landing on it in 2001.

Jupiter

Ceres

Makemake

Haumea

Pluto

Eris

## FIVE DWARF PLANETS

Dwarf planets are almost-round objects that not only orbit the Sun, but do so among other orbiting objects. Four are known in the Kuiper Belt: Eris, Pluto, Makemake, and Haumea. The fifth, Ceres, is in the Asteroid Belt. The discovery of Eris in 2005 led to the introduction of a new class of objects—dwarf planets—in 2006. Before then, Pluto, discovered in 1930, was thought of as a planet.

Ida is 33 miles (54 km) long and orbits the Sun in 4.8 years. Accompanying it is a tiny asteroid named Dactyl, just 1 mile (1.6 km) long, which orbits Ida once every 27 hours.

### METEORITE

Pieces of asteroid that make it to Earth's surface are known as meteorites. Most fall into our planet's oceans and are never found, but more than 30,000 have been recovered by chance or as part of an organized search on land. More than 90 percent of meteorites are made of rock and classed as stony. Second most common are irons, such as this one that fell in Russia in 1947.

# Comets

Way beyond the most distant planet, Neptune, are huge numbers of comets. Together they make the vast Oort Cloud. In this cold and remote part of the Solar System, each comet is a nucleus: a dirty snowball that can be as wide as a city. When a comet leaves the cloud and travels toward the Sun, it undergoes a dramatic change and becomes many times bigger, developing a huge head and two tails. These shrink as the comet speeds away from the Sun and becomes a simple nucleus once more.

## PASSING COMET

About 2,500 comets have been detected traveling through the inner Solar System and around the Sun. Comet Hale-Bopp (right) passed this way in 1997 and was one of the brightest comets seen in Earth's sky in the 20th century. As with all comets, Hale-Bopp's blue gas tail was straight, and the pale tail of dust was curved. It follows a large, elongated orbit and will not appear in our sky again for about 2,500 years or so.

## OORT CLOUD

More than a trillion cometary nuclei make up the spherical Oort Cloud. They are leftover material from when the giant planets formed. Each one of the nuclei follows its own huge orbit around the Sun. The orbits are not in the same plane as those of the planets but at every angle and in every direction. The gravity of a passing star can disturb the nuclei and set them on new orbits, taking them out of the cloud or into the inner Solar System.

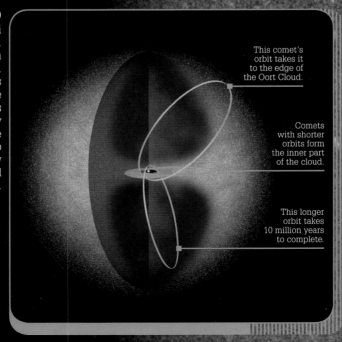

This comet's orbit takes it to the edge of the Oort Cloud.

Comets with shorter orbits form the inner part of the cloud.

This longer orbit takes 10 million years to complete.

## NUCLEUS

A dirty snowball nucleus is a mix of two-thirds snow and one-third silicate-rock dust. Too small to be seen except by visiting spacecraft, fewer than ten nuclei have been imaged. In 2005, the Deep Impact mission encountered the 4.7 mile (7.6 km) long nucleus of Comet Tempel 1 (left). The surface material of a nucleus forms the coma and tails of a comet that travels through the inner Solar System. The nucleus gets smaller each visit until eventually nothing is left.

## COMET'S ORBIT

**1** As a nucleus nears the Sun, its surface snow turns to gas, and dust is released, too. The gas and dust surround the nucleus and form a big head—the coma. Both the gas and dust pushed away from the coma form tails. The tails always point away from the Sun.

Gas tail

Dust tail

Tails grow as the comet approaches the Sun

Tails shrink as comet moves away

Earth's orbit

**Watch a comet travel around the Sun**

## METEORS

Short-lived trails of light seen in Earth's night sky are meteors, also known as shooting stars. Each is produced by a small fragment of comet, or asteroid, as it speeds through our atmosphere. The fragment produces a trail of excited atoms, which glow. Two meteors, part of the Perseid meteor shower, appear as red streaks (top right) in this long-exposure view. A shower of meteors occurs when Earth travels through a trail of dust discarded by a comet.

# Stellar worlds

Stars surround
our planet. We see them
as distant, twinkling points of
light in Earth's night sky. The
brightest of them can be linked by
imaginary lines to make patterns.
Up close, many are like our Sun, but there
are plenty in other colors and sizes, too.
Like humans, stars are born, live, and die,
but their lifetimes last millions or billions
of years. For some, it is a solitary
existence, others have a stellar
companion or two, and some
have a family of planets.

The Bug Nebula,
a dying star

# Constellations

Earth is surrounded by distant stars, which appear as pinpoints of light in our night sky. At first glance these twinkling lights can look very similar, but we tell them apart by linking them with imaginary lines into patterns, like making connect-the-dot pictures in the sky. A pattern and the sky surrounding it is called a constellation, and the whole of the sky surrounding Earth is divided into 88 of them.

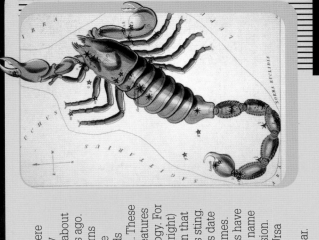

## MYTHICAL CREATURES

Around half of the 88 constellations were formed and used by astronomers living about four thousand years ago. They created patterns in the sky above the Mediterranean lands where they worked. These took the form of creatures from Greek mythology. For instance, Scorpius (right) depicts the scorpion that killed Orion with its sting. Some constellations date from more recent times. Many constellations have two names: a Latin name and a common version. The constellation Ursa Major is commonly called the Great Bear.

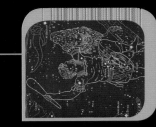

Modern star maps show only stars, but older maps include constellation patterns, too. Orion is usually depicted with a club or sword in his right hand, and a lion's pelt or shield in his left.

The red supergiant star Betelgeuse marks Orion's right shoulder.

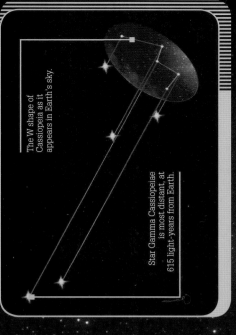

The W shape of Cassiopeia as it appears in Earth's sky.

Star Gamma Cassiopeiae is most distant, at 615 light-years from Earth.

## OPTICAL ILLUSION

The stars in a constellation pattern appear to be the same distance from us. In reality, the stars are vast distances apart and only appear as a group from our viewpoint. If we could travel across space and gaze at them from elsewhere, we'd see them as a different pattern. Seen from Earth, the five main stars of the constellation Cassiopeia make a distinctive W shape, but the stars are unrelated.

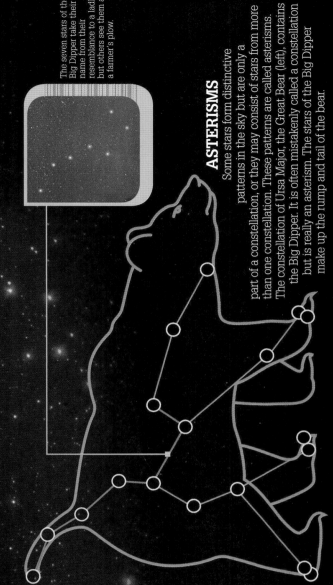

The seven stars of the Big Dipper take their name from their resemblance to a ladle but others see them as a farmer's plow.

## ASTERISMS

Some stars form distinctive patterns in the sky but are only a part of a constellation, or they may consist of stars from more than one constellation. These patterns are called asterisms. The constellation of Ursa Major, the Great Bear (left), contains the Big Dipper. It is often mistakenly called a constellation but is really an asterism. The stars of the Big Dipper make up the rump and tail of the bear.

## ORION, THE HUNTER

The constellation patterns take the shape of a person, creature, or object. Orion, a great hunter in Greek mythology, is very easy to make out. Arms stretch out from a kite shape, which marks his body. Individual stars mark his shoulders and a row of three form his belt. The pink-colored region below his belt is the Orion Nebula, where thousands of stars and some planetary systems are forming.

## BRILLIANT STARS

A constellation pattern is usually drawn using the brightest stars in the night sky. Sirius is the brightest of all and in the constellation Canis Major, also known as the Great Dog. But the brilliance of Sirius and other stars in the sky doesn't represent their true luminosity. Their brightness from Earth is based on how much light the star produces and how far away it is. If Sirius was the same distance as the Sun, it would be twice as big and 25 times as bright.

# Stars

Huge spinning, glowing balls of hot gas are called stars. They are made mainly of hydrogen and partly helium, together with small amounts of other elements. They are born within galaxies from huge clouds of gas and dust. As they age, they move through different life stages, changing their characteristics such as color, temperature, size, and luminosity. A star's development and the length of its life are influenced by one factor above all others—its mass.

## STAR QUALITY

One of the most noticeable things about a star is its luminosity—the amount of light it produces. The most luminous stars emit more than 6 million times the Sun's light; the least produce less than one ten-thousandth. The color of a star's light can reveal its surface temperature. Stars range from the hottest, which are blue and about 72,000°F (40,000°C), through white, yellow, and orange, to the coolest, which are red and about 4,700°F (2,600°C).

## STAR BIRTH

The process of star birth begins when fragments of a vast cloud of gas and dust start to collapse. Gravity pulls material toward the center and eventually a spinning sphere forms. This is called a protostar, the first stage in a star's life. Material in its core becomes increasingly squashed. The temperature and pressure increase, nuclear fusion starts, and the star becomes a teenager. Infant stars are within the dense fingerlike structures (below) in the Eagle Nebula.

## MULTIPLE STARS

Stars are not born alone but in clusters. Over hundreds of millions of years, a cluster separates out and its stars drift apart. The Sun was born in one but is now alone. About half of all nearby stars live alone but others exist alongside star neighbors. The view of the brightest star in the center of this image is deceptive. The star, Pismis 24-1, consists of three stars so close that they appear as one.

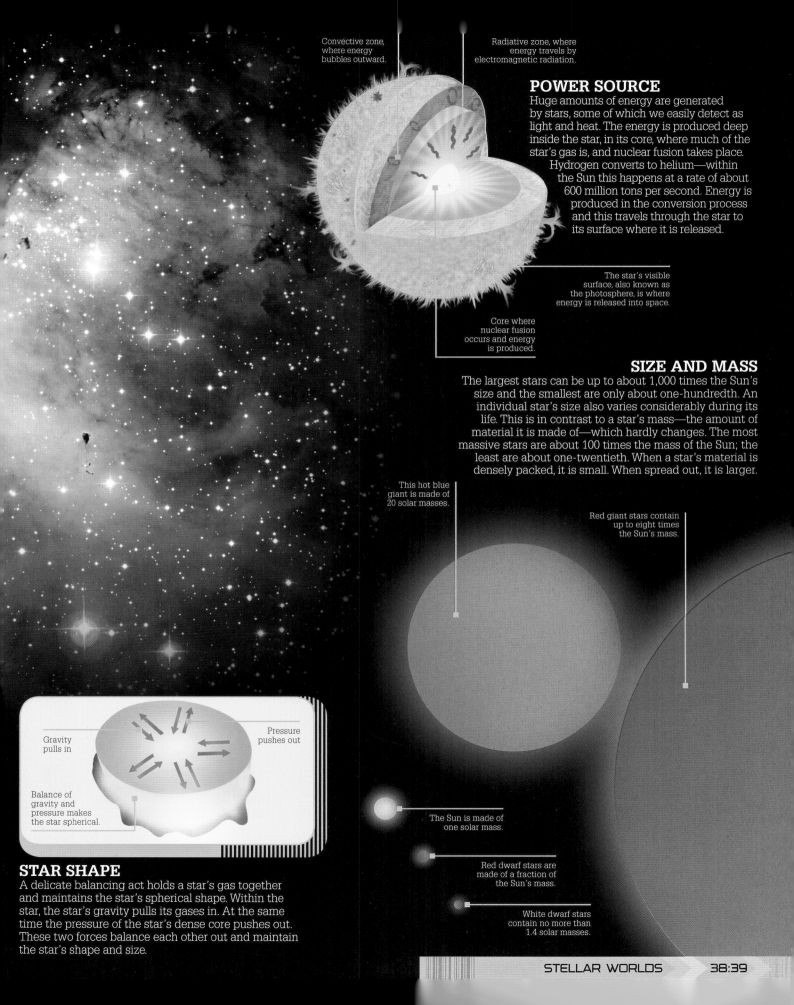

Convective zone, where energy bubbles outward.

Radiative zone, where energy travels by electromagnetic radiation.

## POWER SOURCE

Huge amounts of energy are generated by stars, some of which we easily detect as light and heat. The energy is produced deep inside the star, in its core, where much of the star's gas is, and nuclear fusion takes place. Hydrogen converts to helium—within the Sun this happens at a rate of about 600 million tons per second. Energy is produced in the conversion process and this travels through the star to its surface where it is released.

The star's visible surface, also known as the photosphere, is where energy is released into space.

Core where nuclear fusion occurs and energy is produced.

## SIZE AND MASS

The largest stars can be up to about 1,000 times the Sun's size and the smallest are only about one-hundredth. An individual star's size also varies considerably during its life. This is in contrast to a star's mass—the amount of material it is made of—which hardly changes. The most massive stars are about 100 times the mass of the Sun; the least are about one-twentieth. When a star's material is densely packed, it is small. When spread out, it is larger.

This hot blue giant is made of 20 solar masses.

Red giant stars contain up to eight times the Sun's mass.

Gravity pulls in

Pressure pushes out

Balance of gravity and pressure makes the star spherical.

## STAR SHAPE

A delicate balancing act holds a star's gas together and maintains the star's spherical shape. Within the star, the star's gravity pulls its gases in. At the same time the pressure of the star's dense core pushes out. These two forces balance each other out and maintain the star's shape and size.

The Sun is made of one solar mass.

Red dwarf stars are made of a fraction of the Sun's mass.

White dwarf stars contain no more than 1.4 solar masses.

# Exoplanets

Until the 1990s, the only planets we knew about were the eight in the Solar System. Today, we know of more than 700 and each month we discover more. Called extrasolar planets, or exoplanets, they orbit distant stars, and many astronomers are convinced that some hold life. The search is on to discover more exoplanets, and ones that might be home to extraterrestrial (ET) life.

## FORMATION OF PLANETS

Planets develop from disks of gas and dust material that surround young stars. The material, unused when the central star formed, orbits around the star. Pieces of disk material bump together and eventually form vast bodies—planets. Astronomers found a huge ring of material around the star Fomalhaut (white dot in center) in 2004, and then found a young exoplanet about ten times farther from this star than Saturn is from our Sun.

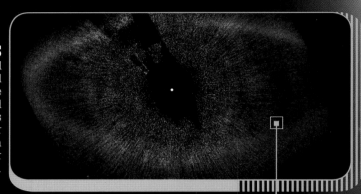

## PLANET HUNTER

Exoplanets are very difficult to find because they are small and next to huge, bright stars. The search method used by the Kepler space telescope is to watch out for the dimming of a star's light as a planet orbits in front of it. Kepler has been working since 2009, constantly monitoring the brightness of 150,000 stars in the Milky Way Galaxy. Within months it found a handful of exoplanets and by 2011 had a list of more than 1,200 potential exoplanets.

This white box pinpoints the location of the exoplanet, named Fomalhaut b.

A radiator covers the telescope tube and keeps the camera detectors inside it cool.

## GLIESE 581

Astronomers think that about five out of every 100 nearby stars have planets orbiting around them. And, like the Sun, some of these stars have more than one planet. Four planets have been discovered orbiting the star Gliese 581 (above). Each discovered planet takes the star's name and a letter. Planet Gliese 581c (right) is five times as massive as Earth, much closer to its star than Earth is to the Sun, and orbits Gliese 581 once every 13 days.

A box of electronics as well as star trackers and an antenna are attached to the part of the telescope containing Kepler's mirror.

Solar panels provide the electric power to run Kepler and its equipment.

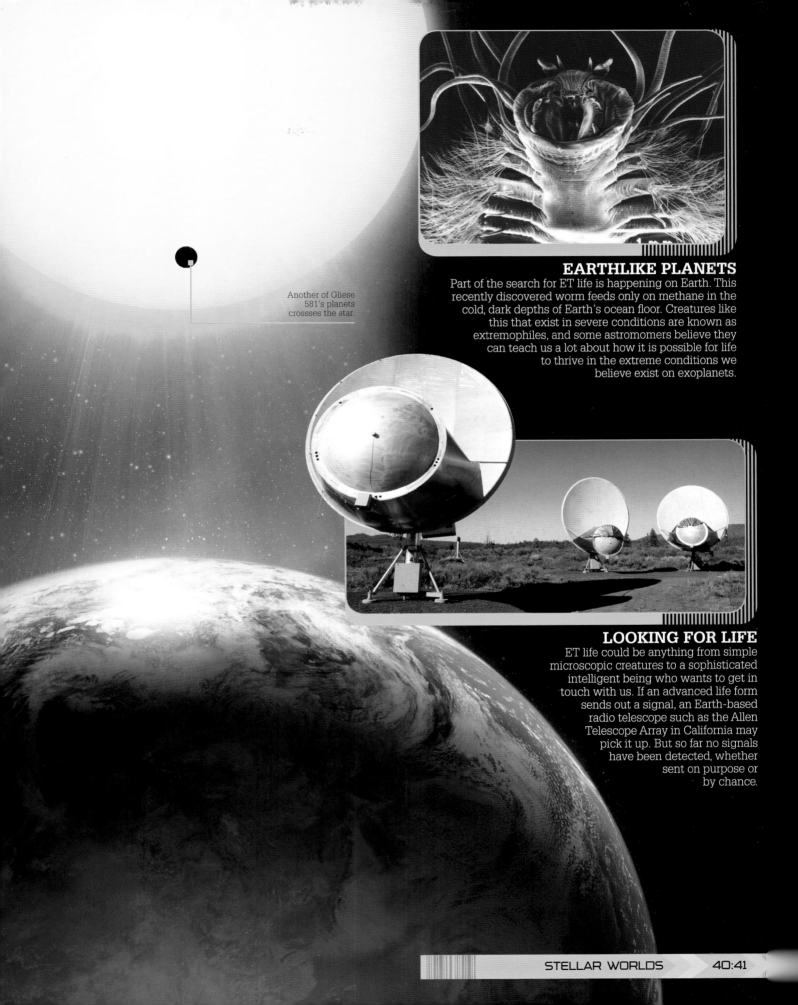

Another of Gliese 581's planets crossses the star.

## EARTHLIKE PLANETS

Part of the search for ET life is happening on Earth. This recently discovered worm feeds only on methane in the cold, dark depths of Earth's ocean floor. Creatures like this that exist in severe conditions are known as extremophiles, and some astromomers believe they can teach us a lot about how it is possible for life to thrive in the extreme conditions we believe exist on exoplanets.

## LOOKING FOR LIFE

ET life could be anything from simple microscopic creatures to a sophisticated intelligent being who wants to get in touch with us. If an advanced life form sends out a signal, an Earth-based radio telescope such as the Allen Telescope Array in California may pick it up. But so far no signals have been detected, whether sent on purpose or by chance.

# Dying stars

Stars have incredibly long lives but they don't live forever. Sunlike stars shine brightly for billions of years before starting their slow dying process, eventually turning into white dwarves. Stars with more mass don't live so long, just a few million years, and face a more dramatic end. They'll abruptly explode as a supernova, and end up as a neutron star or black hole. Material pushed off by all dying stars is eventually recycled and used to make new ones.

## SUPERNOVA!

The stars with more than about eight times the Sun's mass experience a sudden end to their lives. Much of their star material is blasted into space in a colossal explosion. Huge amounts of energy are released and the star becomes an outstandingly bright new star called a supernova. The original star's core is left behind. If made from between about 1.4 and three times the Sun's mass it forms a neutron star. More than this, and it becomes a black hole.

## EXPLOSIVE END

**1** A supernova occurs when the original star's core collapses and a shockwave rips through the star's outer layers. Star material blasted away is then called a supernova remnant (left). It travels at millions of miles per hour into space, leaving the central core behind.

Make a star explode

# In a typical galaxy, one star will go supernova every few hundred years

A clump of cloud material condenses to form stars.

Young stars shine brightly due to nuclear fusion in their cores.

Mature star loses material as it goes through the dying process.

Mixed material is drawn together by gravity and forms a cloud.

Gas and dust shed by stars joins with interstellar material.

## STELLAR RECYCLING

As stars die, they shed gas and dust. Over millions of years this spreads out and mixes with hydrogen gas between the stars. These huge, cold, and dark clouds of mixed material slowly take shape. Gravity continues to pull on the material and dense clumps form within the clouds, and these eventually produce new stars. The stars shine steadily but in time mature and die, and in the process discard material into space, which starts the cycle again.

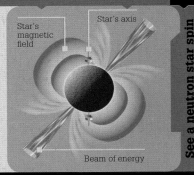

### NEUTRON STAR

**2** Neutron stars are made of more material than the Sun, but packed into a city-sized sphere. They are the smallest, densest stars we can detect. They also spin the fastest, at up to several hundred times a second. One discovered by its energy beams sweeping across space as it spins is called a pulsar.

Star's magnetic field

Star's axis

Beam of energy

See a neutron star spin

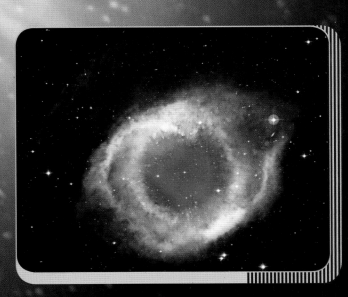

## DEATH OF SUN-LIKE STARS

The Sun is a main sequence star, shining steadily as it converts core hydrogen to helium. All stars pass through this stage and most spend the majority of their life in it. When Sun-like stars run out of hydrogen, they increase in size, cool, change color, and become red giants. As a red giant matures, it pushes off its outer region and forms a planetary nebula (left): a shell of gas and dust surrounding the Earth-sized dying star in the center. Now a white dwarf, the star fades and cools until it becomes a cold, dark cinder in space.

# Discovering space

We have been learning about our space surroundings ever since the first humans looked up and into Earth's sky. Today's astronomers have powerful telescopes both on Earth and in space to help them see more and see farther. They collect light and other forms of energy from space objects. Unmanned spacecraft have been sent out to take a closer look, some traveling around Solar System objects, but others have landed on them and driven across their surfaces, too.

Star trails over Cerro Tololo Inter-American Observatory, Chile

# Exploring from Earth

Astronomers learn about space by collecting and analyzing the energy that space objects emit. The most familiar form of this energy is light, which, along with radio and infrared energy, is collected by telescopes based on Earth. The huge mirrors of optical telescopes gather and focus the light to produce a magnified image of distant objects. Electronic computer chips are used to record the view, and from there it can be displayed on a computer screen.

## HIGH UP
The world's finest optical telescopes are situated on mountain tops, where they get the best view into space. The Keck Telescope, housed inside this protective dome, is one of a dozen telescopes on the summit of Mauna Kea, an extinct volcano on the Big Island of Hawaii. Its mirror is 33 ft (10 m) wide, making this one of the world's largest telescopes and enabling it to collect light from objects in distant space.

Gamma rays

X-rays

Ultraviolet rays

Visible light

Infrared rays

Microwaves

Radio waves

## ELECTROMAGNETIC SPECTRUM
Light and other forms of radiation energy travel in waves. The full range of these waves is called the electromagnetic spectrum. The waves differ in length, and each wavelength has its own name. Light waves and longer wavelengths, such as infrared and radio waves, reach Earth's surface, but shorter ones are absorbed by the atmosphere. Each wavelength can reveal something different about an object, as well as whole new objects not picked up on the other wavelengths.

The James Clerk Maxwell Telescope in Hawaii is the largest telescope that collects submillimeter wavelengths. This type of telescope detects wavelengths that are less than 0.3 in (1 mm) in length.

Since most radio waves reach the ground, radio telescopes can be sited almost anywhere on Earth. The Very Large Array.

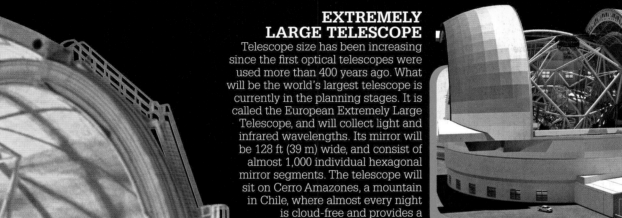

Light collected by the mirror is directed through this central hole to recording instruments.

The mirror is made of glass, and its light-collecting surface, which is regularly cleaned, is coated in aluminum.

The first telescopes
were made in the
early 17th century

## TELESCOPE MIRRORS

The larger a telescope's mirror is, the more light it collects, and the more astronomers see. This 27-ft-(8.2-m-) wide mirror belongs to the Yepun telescope, which is one of four telescopes collectively called the Very Large Telescope at the European Southern Observatory in Paranal, Chile. One-piece mirrors made bigger than this would sag under their own weight, so the largest telescope mirrors, such as that of the Keck, are made of mirror segments that work as one big mirror.

## EXTREMELY LARGE TELESCOPE

Telescope size has been increasing since the first optical telescopes were used more than 400 years ago. What will be the world's largest telescope is currently in the planning stages. It is called the European Extremely Large Telescope, and will collect light and infrared wavelengths. Its mirror will be 128 ft (39 m) wide, and consist of almost 1,000 individual hexagonal mirror segments. The telescope will sit on Cerro Amazones, a mountain in Chile, where almost every night is cloud-free and provides a clear view into the Universe.

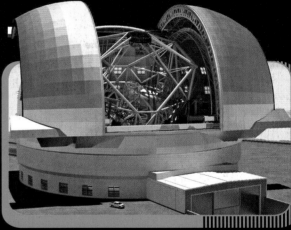

## ANALYZING LIGHT

Light can be split into its constituent rainbow colors by an instrument called a spectrograph. This produces a light spectrum such as this one of the star Aldebaran, the red giant star that marks an eye of the bull in the constellation Taurus. Dark vertical lines crossing the spectrum are caused by chemical elements and tell us what the star's outer layer is made of. Further study can establish other properties such as temperature.

# Space telescopes

Astronomers have been using space-based telescopes for about 40 years. From their position in space, these telescopes can work all day and night, all year through. They collect light from distant objects as well as other wavelengths of energy, including those such as X-rays, which can't penetrate Earth's atmosphere. Collected data is sent to Earth where astronomers study it and turn it into pictures.

Hubble was named in honor of American astronomer Edwin Hubble

## HUBBLE

The Hubble Space Telescope is the best-known space-based telescope. Its 8-ft- (2.4-m-) wide mirror has been collecting optical, ultraviolet, and infrared wavelengths from space objects since 1990. Most space telescopes are on their own in space with no chance of repair or new parts. Hubble is the exception. It was built to be repaired in space, and spacewalking astronauts have made five servicing missions to it.

| Chandra X-ray [High Energy] | Chandra X-ray [Low Energy] | Hubble Optical | Spitzer Infrared |

## COMBINED PICTURE

Images of space objects often combine information collected by telescopes working in different wavelengths. By doing this, astronomers get a more complete picture of the space object. This view of Kepler's supernova remnant, the remains of a star that was observed exploding in 1604, combines X-ray, optical, and infrared data from three different space telescopes: Chandra, Hubble, and Spitzer. Red is microscopic dust, blue and green are hot gas, and yellow denotes a wave of ejected material.

The solar panels convert sunlight into electricity to power the telescope.

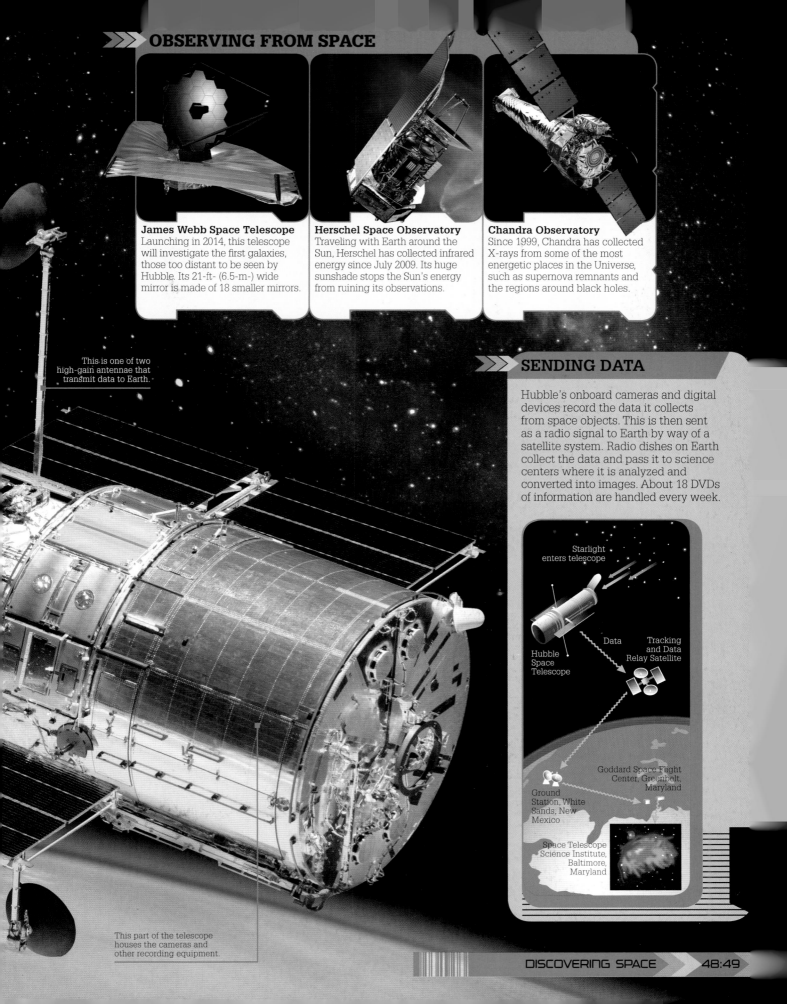

# OBSERVING FROM SPACE

**James Webb Space Telescope**
Launching in 2014, this telescope will investigate the first galaxies, those too distant to be seen by Hubble. Its 21-ft- (6.5-m-) wide mirror is made of 18 smaller mirrors.

**Herschel Space Observatory**
Traveling with Earth around the Sun, Herschel has collected infrared energy since July 2009. Its huge sunshade stops the Sun's energy from ruining its observations.

**Chandra Observatory**
Since 1999, Chandra has collected X-rays from some of the most energetic places in the Universe, such as supernova remnants and the regions around black holes.

This is one of two high-gain antennae that transmit data to Earth.

## SENDING DATA

Hubble's onboard cameras and digital devices record the data it collects from space objects. This is then sent as a radio signal to Earth by way of a satellite system. Radio dishes on Earth collect the data and pass it to science centers where it is analyzed and converted into images. About 18 DVDs of information are handled every week.

Starlight enters telescope

Hubble Space Telescope

Data

Tracking and Data Relay Satellite

Goddard Space Flight Center, Greenbelt, Maryland

Ground Station, White Sands, New Mexico

Space Telescope Science Institute, Baltimore, Maryland

This part of the telescope houses the cameras and other recording equipment.

# Going into space

Anything that goes into space gets there by rocket power. A rocket lifts its cargo off Earth's surface and delivers it into space within minutes.

The cargo can be astronauts, a spacecraft traveling into the Solar System, or a craft such as a satellite that will orbit around Earth.

Rockets are used for a single space journey but between 1981 and 2011, five Space Shuttles made regular trips into space and back.

## ROCKET STAGES

The simplest rockets are one-stage rockets; they have one set of engines and fuel, and these are ignited on the ground. Many rockets are multistage, meaning they have engines and fuel in various parts, or stages, of the rocket. These stages are used in turn, one after the other, and as one stage is used up, this part of the rocket is jettisoned, which makes the remaining rocket lighter. The first stage is the base of the rocket and its engines are ignited on the launch pad. A second, and at times a third stage too are ignited above the ground once earlier stages have done their job. The last stage releases the rocket's cargo, known as its payload, into space.

Payload released in space.

Once in space, the stage two engines cut out and the payload is released.

Stage two engines ignite and propel the rocket into space.

Payload

Second stage

First stage

Stage one falls away once its fuel has been used up and its work is done.

The complete rocket is lifted off the ground by the stage one engines.

It is generally accepted that space starts at 62 miles (100 km) above Earth

## ROCKET POWER

In the nose of this Soyuz FG rocket is a craft with three astronauts heading for the International Space Station (ISS). Fuel burned in the rocket's engines produces gases. As these gases speed out of the bottom of the rocket, the craft is forced upward and away from Earth. The more fuel burned, the lighter the rocket becomes and the faster it goes. At a speed of 7 miles (11.3 km) per second it escapes Earth's gravity.

## SPACE SHUTTLE

The reusable Space Shuttle consisted of three main parts. The orbiter, which carried the astronauts, was the only part to travel into space. The two others—the huge fuel tank for the orbiter's engines, and booster rockets used in the liftoff—fell back to Earth within minutes of the launch. The orbiter returned like a glider; as it landed, a drag chute helped bring it to a stop.

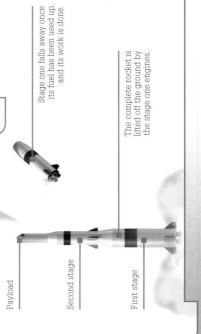

## LAUNCH SITES

**Key**

1. Vandenberg, California
2. Cape Canaveral, Florida
3. Kourou, French Guiana
4. Baikonur, Kazakhstan
5. Sriharikota Island, India
6. Juquan, Inner Mongolia
7. Xichang, China
8. Tanegashima, Japan

Rockets start their journey into space at one of 30 or so launch sites, eight of which are shown here. The sites consist of launch pads as well as buildings for the preparation, servicing, and launch of spacecraft. Baikonur is the largest and has been in continuous use since 1957. European rockets launch from Kourou.

## LAUNCHPAD

A launchpad is the exact place a rocket launches from and the area immediately around this. Launchpad 39A in Florida (above) was used to launch Saturn V rockets and Space Shuttles. The rocket is transported to its pad and, once fixed into its upright, launch position, it is fueled. A launch tower at the rocket's side provides access until the engines are fired and the rocket takes off

## SPACESHIPONE

A third form of space transportation—the reusable spaceplane—is being prepared for space travel. Built by commercial companies, it will carry passengers on short space trips. The first craft of this type to make a manned spaceflight was SpaceShipOne in 2004 (above). The White Knight aircraft carried SpaceShipOne to 9 miles (15 km) above Earth, and then released it. SpaceShipOne's rockets ignited and burned for about 80 seconds, sending it soaring into space before it glided back to Earth.

White Knight

SpaceShipOne

# Robot explorers

About 100 unmanned robotic spacecraft
have successfully explored our Solar System
for us. The craft are designed for individual
missions but all are about the size of a bus,
or family car, and have power, computers,
tools, and instruments on board to collect
information and beam it back to Earth.
They don't come back once their work
is done, but stay where they've landed or
continue to travel through space.

## TO SATURN

One of the biggest craft to
explore the Solar System is
Cassini-Huygens, which arrived at
Saturn in June 2004. A few months
after arrival, the small craft Huygens
separated from Cassini and descended to
the surface of Saturn's largest moon, Titan,
beaming back its findings to Earth. Since
then, the main craft, Cassini, has orbited
Saturn, orienting itself so that its
12 instruments study the planet,
its rings, and moons.

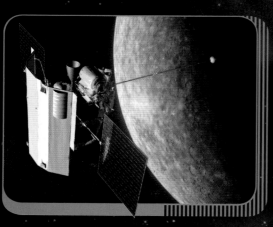

## MESSENGER

Before moving into orbit around the planet Mercury
in March 2011, the Messenger spacecraft flew past
it three times, Venus twice, and Earth once to slow
the craft down. Once in orbit, Messenger completed
a circuit of the planet every 12 hours. Onboard
cameras photographed the entire surface, revealing
huge regions of Mercury never seen before, and a
laser altimeter collected data to produce a surface
map. Messenger's huge sunshade protected the
craft from the Sun's harsh rays as it worked.

## NEW HORIZONS

The New Horizons spacecraft is due
to arrive at the dwarf planet Pluto in
July 2015, after a journey lasting almost
11.5 years. As it approaches Pluto and
then flies by one side of it, New Horizons'
cameras will give us our first detailed view
of this distant world. It will then move
on to investigate a Kuiper Belt object.
Throughout its mission, antenna dishes in
Australia, Spain, and the United States
keep the craft in touch with Earth.

## COMET CHASER

The Rosetta mission is on its way to comet Churyumov-Gerasimenko. On arrival in August 2014 it will be the first craft to orbit around a cometary nucleus. Rosetta will work alongside the nucleus for about 15 months as the comet travels along its path around the Sun. It will monitor changes in the surface of the nucleus as the comet approaches the Sun, travels around it, and then moves away. A small landing craft called Philae, released by Rosetta onto the nucleus, will provide more information.

## RETURNING SAMPLES

A small number of robotic missions have involved craft that return to Earth with a sample of space material, such as soil from the Moon or rocky grains from an asteroid. In January 2006, the Stardust mission returned a capsule that included particles of comet Wild 2. Upon opening the capsule, the scientists found the particles had been successfully captured within the sample collector (above).

## PALE BLUE DOT

Voyager 1 left Earth in 1977 and headed off to Jupiter. After investigating the planet and its neighbor, Saturn, it continued to travel farther away from the Sun. In February 1990, when it was about 4 billion miles (6.5 billion km) away, Voyager 1 looked back and took this image of its home planet. Earth appears as an insignificant small, pale blue dot in the vastness of space. Voyager 1 is now about 10.9 billion miles (17.5 billion km) away, making it the most distant craft from Earth.

# Landers and rovers

Unmanned craft have landed on six Solar System worlds: Venus and Mars; our Moon and Saturn's moon Titan; and two asteroids, Eros and Itokawa. When the craft arrive, they either stay still on the spot where they landed, or they rove around. Stationary landers can only investigate their vicinity. Rovers, however, can drive over long stretches of land, stopping from time to time to take photographs and make on-the-spot investigations.

## OPPORTUNITY LANDS

**Make Opportunity land on the surface of Mars**

**1** Upon arrival on Mars, a parachute slowed the aeroshell's descent. As it fell, the aeroshell released Opportunity in its airbag casing. The airbags inflated, allowing the craft to bounce and roll across the surface. Once at a stop, the airbags deflated, and the craft got ready to rove.

## OPPORTUNITY

The most successful rover is Opportunity (right). It arrived on Mars in 2004, inside a type of craft called an aeroshell. Its twin, Spirit, was already on the other side of the planet. Opportunity touched down on Meridiani Planum, a low-lying cratered plain, which it is still exploring. The rover looks across the plain using cameras on its mast. Instruments on a jointed arm at the front of its body investigate the surface.

569146-8/0
S/N0001 REV

The equipment deck, with solar panels on its upper surface, provides power and protects Opportunity's box-shaped body underneath, which contains a computer, radios, and batteries.

The Rock Abrasion Tool, often just called RAT, rotates its grinding wheels to remove dust and weathered rock, in order to analyze fresh rock underneath.

## FIRST ROVERS

Rovers have been to just two places, the Moon and Mars. The first to go were identical craft Lunokhod 1 and 2 (below) which worked on the Moon for fifteen months in the early 1970s. They explored almost 31 miles (50 km) of the lunar surface, returning tens of thousands of images and testing its soil at different places. Sojourner became the first Mars rover in 1997.

It takes about 10 minutes for a message from Opportunity to reach Earth

## OPPORTUNITY EXPLORES

**2** When Opportunity travels, its arm is tucked in. Upon stopping next to a targeted rock, the arm unfolds until it is next to the rock's surface. The arm works like a human's, bending and moving shoulder, elbow, and wrist joints. At the end are tools that can grind, image, and analyze the rock.

**Explore the surface of Mars with Opportunity**

This antenna is used for direct communication with Earth. It receives commands and software updates, and returns data from the cameras and other instruments.

Each of the six wheels is about 10 in (26 cm) in diameter and has its own motor. The wheel surface can grip both in soft sand and on hard rock.

## LANDERS

The first craft to land on a world outside of Earth was Luna 2, which impacted the lunar surface in 1959. During the 1970s, landers arrived on Venus and Mars, sending back the first close-up images of these planets. In 2005, Huygens (above) landed on Titan and revealed smooth rocks, shaped by flowing liquid, on the surface beneath a deep and dense nitrogen atmosphere.

# Human travelers

Men and women who travel into space are called astronauts. Their space trips usually last just a week or two, but some stay for months at a time. The weightless conditions in space affect everything they do, from their day's work to eating their lunch. Astronauts are there now, orbiting Earth in a huge spacecraft that they built called the International Space Station. Some astronauts have traveled farther, as far as the Moon, and explored its gray, desolate surface.

Apollo 17 astronaut
Harrison Schmitt
on the Moon

# Astronauts

Since 1961, more than 500 astronauts have traveled into space aboard rockets or Space Shuttles. Nearly all have traveled only as far as the part of space immediately above Earth. The exceptions are the 24 who journeyed as far as the Moon. Astronauts are employed by national space agencies, although in recent years a small number of private individuals have traveled into space, too.

## TRAINING
Astronauts have come from about 40 different nations but all prepare for spaceflight in the same way. They spend many hours in the classroom as well as handling space equipment and working on life-size simulations. Their first experience of weightlessness is aboard a specially modified plane that follows a special path called a parabolic loop. As the plane falls downward on the loop, the astronauts inside feel weightless and float around.

## JOB REQUIREMENTS
Astronauts are chosen for their specific qualities. They usually have university or equivalent qualifications in a science-based subject, are about 27 to 37 years old, and are mentally and physically fit. These seven astronauts have successfully completed their training and are about to board the silver Astrovan. It will take them to the launchpad where Space Shuttle Atlantis is waiting to carry them to the International Space Station.

## PIONEERS

**First in space**
The first person in space was the Russian astronaut Yuri Gagarin. On April 12, 1961, he orbited Earth once in his Soyuz space capsule. His journey lasted just 108 minutes.

**First woman**
Only about a tenth of all astronauts have been women and nearly all were American. In 1963, Russian Valentina Tereshkova became the first woman in space.

**Oldest astronaut**
In 1962, John Glenn became the first American to orbit Earth. The next flight he took was in 1998, at the age of 77, making him the oldest astronaut to fly.

**Most time**
Russian Sergei Krikalev journeyed into space six times. He stayed for a total of 803 days, 9 hours, and 39 minutes, spending more time in space than anyone else.

## SPACE TOURISTS

Dennis Tito was the first private citizen to pay to go into space, which made him the first space tourist. In 2001, this American businessman's weeklong trip aboard the International Space Station cost him about $20 million. To date, there have been fewer than ten space tourists, but commercial businesses are selling tickets for future trips into space. In the next few years SpaceShipTwo will carry passengers on regular two-and-a-half-hour trips to the edge of space and back.

## WEIGHTLESSNESS

A key difference between being on Earth and being in space is the sensation of weightlessness that astronauts feel. Gravity is pulling them to Earth, but because they are moving horizontally around Earth at the same time, they feel weightless, giving them the feeling of constantly falling through space. Astronauts monitor themselves to see how it affects their bodies. Muscles don't have to work as hard and weaken, and the heart doesn't have to pump as powerfully to send blood around the body.

## ANIMALS IN SPACE

Animals flew in space before the first human astronauts. They were sent to see how living creatures coped with spaceflight. The largest animals ever sent were dogs, monkeys, and chimpanzees. In 1957, a dog called Laika (top right) traveled inside Sputnik 2 and became the first creature to complete an orbit of Earth. Chimpanzees were chosen because of their similar genetic makeup to humans. The first, Ham (bottom right), flew in 1961 to test equipment prior to the first manned American mission. Since those early days, other living creatures such as mice, snails, honeybees, fish, and ants have traveled into space.

# Spacewalk

Astronauts that venture outside their spacecraft are described as being on an extravehicular activity, more commonly known as a spacewalk. About 200 astronauts have spacewalked, making more than 700 individual walks between them, usually to work on their craft. The first, in March 1965 by Russian Alexei Leonov, lasted only ten minutes. Today walks regularly last about seven hours. Most spacewalks have been spent constructing and maintaining the International Space Station (ISS).

## SUITED UP

Spacewalking astronauts wear special clothing and are secured to stop them from floating away. Their spacesuit and helmet protect them from space. They also provide an Earth-like environment and oxygen to breathe. The suit, officially called the Extravehicular Mobility Unit (EMU), consists of a semirigid top and pants that fit together. Suits kept aboard the ISS come in standard sizes and are used about 25 times before being retired.

## LIFE SUPPORT

Oxygen for breathing is kept in a backpack called the Primary Life Support System, and carbon dioxide exhaled by the astronaut is recycled here too. Mountaineering-style tethers up to 25 ft (7.6 m) in length secure the astronaut to his craft. Should these fail, jet thrusters on a system called SAFER worn at the base of the backpack can be activated to fly the astronaut back to safety.

Beneath the spacesuit an astronaut wears a one-piece undergarment. Cool water flows through thin plastic tubes laced in the fabric of the underwear to keep the astronaut cool by removing body heat.

Astronaut Stephen Robinson is secured to the foot restraint of Canadarm2 on the ISS. The robotic arm is controlled by an astronaut inside the station.

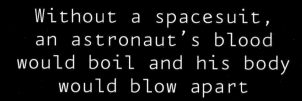

Without a spacesuit, an astronaut's blood would boil and his body would blow apart

## DOORWAY TO SPACE

Preparing for a spacewalk takes several hours. Inside a small sealed room called an airlock, nonspacewalking astronauts help spacewalking astronauts dress. Then left alone, the suited astronauts breathe pure oxygen and get used to reduced air pressure before opening a hatch and moving into space. They return through the hatch feet first as this astronaut is doing (above).

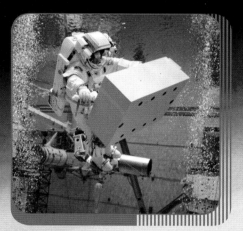

## ON-EARTH TRAINING

Astronauts usually spacewalk in pairs and the two train together in a giant water pool on Earth. Working underwater is the best way to simulate the weightless conditions they will find in space. In the tank, they work on full-scale models of the ISS parts they will be working on in space. For every one hour of spacewalking, they spend seven hours training in the water.

## TOOLS

Astronauts have spent more than 1,000 hours working on the ISS. Their main tool on these missions is the pistol grip tool, a battery-powered cordless drill, useful for a variety of tasks. Every tool is specially designed to be gripped by gloved hands, and to work in varying temperatures and weightless conditions. They are tethered to stop them from floating away.

# On the Moon

The only place that humans have been to outside of Earth is the Moon. Twenty-four men have traveled there, and 12 of them set foot upon its surface. The moonwalkers were all American, and journeyed there in six separate Apollo missions: the first in 1969 and the last in 1972. Between them they spent more than 300 hours on the Moon, 80 of which were spent outside their craft, exploring the desolate surface.

## PREPARING TO LAND

More than 20 unmanned craft were sent to the Moon to collect information that would be helpful in planning manned missions. Lunar Orbiter craft (above) photographed the surface so landing sites could be chosen. Later, manned missions Apollo 8 and Apollo 10 orbited the Moon and approached its surface to test the Apollo spacecraft.

## EXPLORING THE SURFACE

The six landing missions touched down in separate locations. The astronauts collected rock and soil, took photographs, and set up experiments to record data long after they had returned home. Three missions had the benefit of exploring with a Lunar Rover (below), but they stayed within 6 miles (10 km) of their Lunar Module in case the Rover broke down. Any farther and their oxygen would have run out before they made it back.

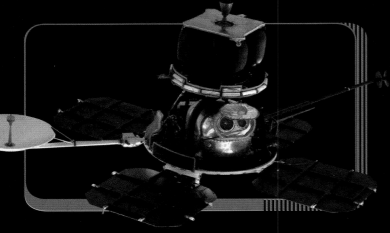

The astronauts had enough oxygen in their backpacks for up to nine hours outside their Lunar Module.

The high-gain antenna, which transmitted color TV signals to Earth, was switched on when the Rover was stationary.

The battery-powered Rover carried two astronauts, their tools, and the rock and soil samples they collected.

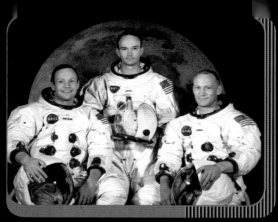

## FIRST TO THE MOON

The Apollo 11 mission was the first to land astronauts on the Moon. Neil Armstrong (left) and Buzz Aldrin (right) traveled to the surface in the Lunar Module, Eagle. They landed on July 21, 1969. Neil was first to leave Eagle and walk on to the Moon's surface. While he and Buzz were on the Moon, the third crew member, Michael Collins, orbited in the Command and Service Module.

The Lunar Rover had a top speed of 11.5 mph (18.5 kph)

6. CSM heads to Earth with three astronauts. LM has already been jettisoned.

5. Upper, ascent part of LM launches away from Moon to rejoin CSM.

4. LM descends to the Moon's surface with two astronauts.

7. The Service Module already jettisoned, the Command Module approaches Earth, parachuting into the Pacific Ocean.

2. CSM is docked to LM; they head for the Moon.

1. Saturn V rocket launches Apollo craft with three astronauts and releases it into Earth orbit.

## THE JOURNEY

The Apollo craft carrying men to the Moon started its journey in the nose cone of a Saturn V rocket. Once released into space, the craft orbited Earth before heading to the Moon. It consisted of three parts: the Command and Service Modules (CSM) which were combined for much of the trip, and the Lunar Module (LM), the only part to reach the Moon's surface.

## MOON ROCK

About 2,200 samples of rock and soil were collected from the Moon. Astronauts used tongs, scoops, hammers, and core tubes pushed into the ground to get subsurface material. Many of the rocks were breccia, produced when asteroids crashed into the young Moon. Others were basalts formed from volcanic lava that seeped through the Moon's crust to the surface.

## LUNAR MODULE

Astronauts landed on the Moon's surface in a Lunar Module. The upper part of the module was their home for the three days spent on the Moon. When it was time to leave, the upper part blasted into space, leaving the lower part behind. It then rejoined the Command and Service Module orbiting the Moon. In this picture the Apollo 16 Lunar Module (known as Intrepid) is flying over the surface prior to landing.

# Space home

The International Space Station (ISS) is the biggest artificial object to orbit Earth. This football-field-sized spacecraft has been the home and workplace for astronauts since 2000. Too big to be launched in one piece, the ISS was constructed in space. Assembly began in 1998 and has involved more than 100 parts being delivered in about 40 launches. The station is an international collaboration of 16 countries; more than 200 astronauts from at least 15 different nations have worked there.

## THE ISS

A fretwork construction called the truss runs the length of the ISS. This supports two sets of huge solar arrays and, between them, a system of interconnected modules. The modules provide the living and work areas, including three laboratories: Destiny, Kibo, and Columbus. Inside, the ISS is big enough to accommodate six astronauts for weeks to months at a time. The ISS travels at 17,400 mph (28,000 kph), orbiting Earth every 90 minutes at an altitude of about 240 miles (390 km).

## REACHING THE ISS

Astronauts travel to the ISS in a capsule launched from Earth by a Soyuz rocket. After docking temporarily with the station, the Soyuz capsule (far right) returns home with a previous crew. Until mid-2011, astronauts were ferried to and from the station by space shuttle, too. The shuttle was also responsible for carrying most of the ISS's major parts into space. Small parts and other supplies such as food usually arrive by unmanned Progress craft (right).

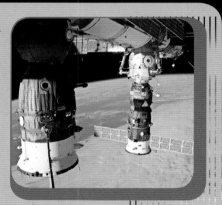

This drum-shaped module is the smaller of the two modules that make up the Japanese experiment laboratory Kibo.

Canadarm2 glides on rails that stretch the entire length of the central truss, which forms the backbone of the ISS.

Solar arrays convert sunlight into electricity, which is stored in batteries. They turn to face the Sun as the ISS travels.

# FIRST SPACE STATIONS

**Salyut**
The first space station was the Russian craft Salyut 1, launched in 1971. It was home to a crew of three. More Salyuts followed, but Salyut 7 (above), was the last.

**Skylab**
The American station Skylab orbited Earth from 1973 to 1979. The last of its three crews left in 1974. It was destroyed after being guided into Earth's atmosphere.

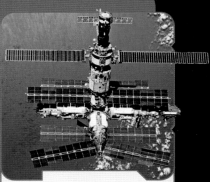

**Mir**
The Russian craft Mir was the first station constructed in space. It was one-quarter the size of the ISS, and was occupied almost continuously between 1987 and 2000.

More than 2,000 spacewalking hours have been spent assembling the ISS

## CANADARM2

**1** The 57 ft (17 m) long Canadarm2 robotic arm works outside the ISS moving equipment and astronauts. It has similar movement to a human arm, with joints to allow it to bend and turn. The arm is operated by an astronaut from Destiny's control desk, or from the cupola, an observation area.

Move an astronaut into place with Canadarm2

## WORKING OUTSIDE THE ISS

**2** All major components of the ISS are now in space, and have been fitted together by spacewalking astronauts (right). In up to four separate walks they move a newly arrived part into position, and then connect it to the existing structure.

Watch an astronaut on a spacewalk

# Living in space

Astronauts go to the ISS to work. They may work on the station itself, carrying out construction or maintenance tasks, which often means spacewalking outside the ISS. At other times they carry out experiments in one of the station's laboratories. Unlike employees on Earth, who go home at the end of their day, astronauts live at their workplace. When not busy with jobs, they do the same things they do back home, such as eating, sleeping, relaxing, and enjoying themselves.

## DAILY SCHEDULE

ISS astronauts use the clock rather than the Sun to rule their day because they experience sunrise and sunset about 16 times a day. Their daily schedule includes up to nine working hours, as well as set times for meals, exercise, and housekeeping tasks. Free time is spent taking photos, watching DVDs, or listening to music. Astronauts can also enjoy the view of Earth by looking out the windows.

## STAYING ALIVE

Everything astronauts do in space is affected by weightlessness. This includes all the normal things done on Earth to stay alive, such as eating, drinking, sleeping, and going to the bathroom. Ready-prepared foods packed in cans or bags float free if not held down. Sleeping astronauts and those using the bathroom are strapped in place to stop them from floating around. Toilet waste is sucked rather than flushed away.

## KEEPING FIT

Astronauts have two daily sessions on the ISS exercise equipment. This is to work their muscles, which aren't ordinarily used in the weightless environment. There are three types of equipment to choose from: a treadmill, an exercise bike, and the Resistive Exercise Device (right), which is similar to a weight-training system on Earth.

...member who uses a vacuum cleaner to stop the cut hair from floating around.

## INDOOR WORK

Astronauts working inside the ISS are usually found in one of its three laboratories: Destiny, Columbus, and Kibo. They carry out experiments such as plant growth and testing how the human body copes in space. The results are useful in planning future astronaut travel. Some experiments are carried out in a small transparent portable laboratory. This is the glovebox, so named because astronauts put their hands into gloves, which are part of the sealed box.

STAYING IN TOUCH

The ISS and its astronauts are monitored around the clock by teams of scientists, engineers, and astronauts in two flight control rooms: this one in Houston, and a second in Russia. The team members are called flight controllers, and each is assigned a specific function, for instance monitoring the spacewalks or speaking with the crew on behalf of the whole team. The controllers stay in touch with the ISS by means of a network of communication satellites in orbit around Earth.

### Active galaxy
A galaxy that emits a huge amount of energy, much of which comes from material falling into a supermassive black hole at its center.

### Antenna
An aerial in the shape of a rod, dish, or array for receiving or transmitting radio waves.

### Asteroid
A small rocky body orbiting the Sun. Most are in the Asteroid Belt, also called the Main Belt, between Mars and Jupiter.

### Astronaut
A man or woman who travels into space.

### Astronomer
Someone who studies the stars and planets and other objects in space.

### Atmosphere
The layer of gases held around a planet, moon, or star by its gravity.

### Atom
The smallest particle of a chemical element.

### Big Bang
The event that created the Universe 13.7 billion years ago.

### Black hole
The remains of a star, or galaxy core that has collapsed in on itself (often called a supermassive black hole). Black holes have gravity so strong that no matter, light, or radiation can escape from them.

### Brightness
A measure of the light of a star. Astronomers measure brightness in two ways: as seen from Earth, and the amount of light a star emits.

### Cluster
A group of galaxies or stars held together by gravity.

### Comet
A small snow-and-dust body. Those traveling near the Sun develop a huge head and two tails.

### Constellation
An imaginary pattern made from stars, and the region of sky around them. Earth's sky is divided into 88 constellations.

### Convection
The transfer of heat by movement, for example, when warmer gas rises and cooler gas falls within a star.

### Crater
A bowl-shaped hollow on the surface of a planet or moon.

### Dark energy
A mysterious form of energy that makes up 72 percent of the Universe and is responsible for the acceleration of the expansion of the Universe.

### Dark matter
Matter that does not emit energy but whose gravity affects its surroundings. It makes up 23 percent of the Universe.

### Density
A measure of how tightly the mass of an object is packed into its volume.

### Dwarf galaxy
A small galaxy containing only a million to several billion stars.

### Dwarf planet
An almost-round body that orbits the Sun as part of a belt of objects.

### Eclipse
The effect achieved when one body such as a star, planet, or moon is in the shadow of another.

### Electromagnetic radiation
A range of energy waves that travel through space. They include gamma rays, X-rays, ultraviolet, light, infrared, microwaves, and radio waves.

### Element
A basic substance of nature such as hydrogen or oxygen.

### Elliptical
Shaped like an ellipse, which is an elongated circle or sphere.

### Exoplanet
A planet that orbits around a star other than the Sun. Sometimes called an extrasolar planet.

### Extraterrestrial
Something or somebody that comes from somewhere other than Earth.

### Fly-by
A close encounter made with a Solar System object by a spacecraft that flies past it.

### Galaxy
An enormous grouping of stars, gas, dust, and dark matter held together by gravity.

### Giant planet
One of the four largest Solar System planets. In order of decreasing size and distance from the Sun they are Jupiter, Saturn, Uranus, and Neptune.

### Gravity
A force of attraction found throughout the Universe. The greater the mass of a body, the greater its gravitational pull.

### Helium
The second most abundant chemical element in the Universe.

### Hydrogen
The lightest and most abundant chemical element in the Universe.

### Infrared
A form of energy, primarily heat energy, that travels in waves longer than light waves.

### Kuiper Belt object
A rock-and-ice body orbiting the Sun within the Kuiper Belt, beyond the orbit of Neptune.

### Lander
A spacecraft that lands on the surface of a planet, moon, asteroid, or comet.

### Lava
Molten rock released through a volcano or crack in the surface of a planet or moon.

### Light-year
A unit of distance. One light-year is the distance light travels in one year—5.88 trillion miles (9.46 trillion km).

### Luminosity
The total amount of energy emitted in one second by a star.

### Lunar
Relating to the Moon; for example, the "lunar surface" is the surface of the Moon.

### Magnetic field
Any place where a magnetic force can be measured, such as around Earth.

### Mare
A smooth plain of solidified lava on the Moon. (plural: maria)

**Mass**
A measure of the amount of material (matter) a body is made of.

**Matter**
The substance that things are made of.

**Meteor**
A short-lived streak of light produced by a small piece of comet, or asteroid, as it speeds through Earth's upper atmosphere.

**Meteorite**
A piece of rock, metal, or rock-and-metal mix that lands on a planet or moon's surface.

**Methane**
An element made of one atom of carbon and four of hydrogen.

**Microwave**
A form of energy that travels in waves measuring between 0.3 in (1 mm) and 12 in (30 cm).

**Milky Way**
The galaxy we live in. Also, the name given to the band of stars that crosses Earth's sky and is our view into the galaxy's disk.

**Module**
A complete unit of a spacecraft; for instance, Kibo is a module of the International Space Station.

**Moon**
A rock or rock-and-ice body that orbits a planet or an asteroid.

**Nebula**
A cloud of gas and dust in space. Some emit their own light, others shine by reflecting light, and those that block out light from background stars appear dark. (plural: nebulae)

**Neutron star**
A dense, compact star formed from the core of an exploding star. It is about the size of a city but consists of the same mass as the Sun.

**Nuclear reaction**
The process in which elements inside a star produce other elements and energy is released. For example, hydrogen nuclei fuse to produce helium, and energy, such as heat and light, is emitted in the process.

**Nucleus**
The body of a comet, the central part of a galaxy, or the central core of an atom. (plural: nuclei)

**Oort Cloud**
A sphere consisting of more than a trillion comets that surrounds the planetary part of the Solar System.

**Orbit**
The path that a natural or artificial body makes around another more massive body.

**Orbiter**
A spacecraft that orbits around a space body such as a planet or asteroid.

**Photosphere**
The outer, visible layer of the Sun, or another star.

**Planet**
A massive, round body that orbits around a star and shines by reflecting the star's light.

**Planetary nebula**
A colorful expanding cloud of ejected gas and dust surrounding the remains of a dying star.

**Polar**
Relating to the north and south poles of an object.

**Pressure**
The force felt when something presses against a surface.

**Protostar**
A very young star in the early stages of formation, before nuclear reactions start in its core.

**Pulsar**
A rapidly rotating neutron star from which we receive brief pulses of energy as the star spins.

**Radiation**
Energy traveling as electromagnetic waves such as infrared or light.

**Rocky planet**
One of the four planets closest to the Sun and made of rock and metal. In order of distance from the Sun they are Mercury, Venus, Earth, and Mars.

**Rover**
A spacecraft that moves across the surface of a planet or moon.

**Satellite**
An artifical object deliberately placed in orbit around Earth, or another Solar System body. Also, another name for a moon or any space object orbiting a more massive one.

**Solar**
Relating to the Sun. For example, the "solar temperature" is the temperature of the Sun.

**Solar nebula**
The spinning cloud of gas and dust that formed into the Solar System.

**Solar System**
The Sun and the objects that orbit it, including eight planets and many smaller bodies.

**Spacesuit**
The all-in-one sealed clothing unit worn by astronauts when outside their craft in space.

**Spacewalk**
An excursion by an astronaut outside a craft when in space, or on a world outside Earth.

**Star**
A huge sphere of hot, luminous gas that generates energy by nuclear reactions.

**Supercluster**
A grouping of galaxy clusters held together by gravity.

**Supernova**
A star that explodes and leaves a supernova remnant behind, and whose core can become a neutron star, pulsar, or black hole. (plural: supernovae)

**Ultraviolet**
A form of energy that travels in waves. Ultraviolet waves are emitted by the Sun and can cause sunburn.

**Universe**
Everything that exists: all time, and all space, and everything in it.

**Volume**
The amount of space an object occupies.

**Wavelength**
The distance between the peaks or troughs in waves of energy.

**Weightlessness**
The sensation experienced by astronauts in space because traveling in space is like constantly falling through space.

**X-ray**
A ray of energy that travels in waves, shorter in wavelength than light waves.

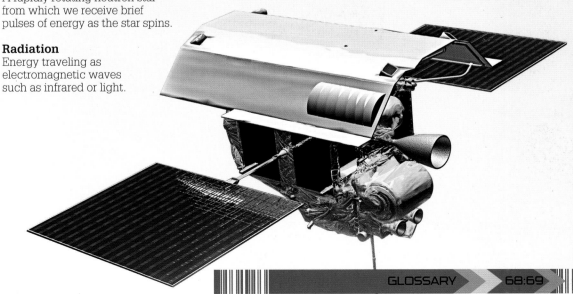

# Index

The publisher would like to thank Katie Knutton for additional artworks, Charlotte Webb for proofreading, Jackie Brind for the index, and John Searcy for Americanization.

Carole Stott would like to dedicate this book to Luke, Max, and Abigail, and anyone else interested in the Universe around them. And not forgetting Steven: it was a pleasure to work with you on your first solo mission.

The publisher would like to thank the following for their kind permission to reproduce their photographs:
(**Key:** a-above; b-below/bottom; c-center; l-left; r-right; t-top)

**1 NASA:** ESA, and J. Maĺz Apell·niz (Instituto de Astrofĺsica de Andalucĺa, Spain). **2 NASA:** JPL-Caltech / University of Arizona (tr); Erich Karkoschka, University of Arizona (tl); JPL / USGS (bl). **2-3 NASA:** JPL (t); JPL / University of Arizona (b). **3 Science Photo Library:** Friedrich Saurer (cr). **4 Corbis:** Sergei Ilnitsky / epa (l). **NASA:** JPL-Caltech and The Hubble Heritage Team (STScI / AURA) (tc); JPL / Ames Research Center (tr). **5 Corbis:** Roger Ressmeyer (tc, clb). **Moonpans.com:** Mike Constantine (tr). **NASA:** ESA and the Hubble SM4 ERO Team (tl). **6-7 NASA:** JPL-Caltech and The Hubble Heritage Team (STScI / AURA). **8 NASA:** ESA, R. O'Connell (University of Virginia), F. Paresce (National Institute for Astrophysics, Bologna, Italy), E. Young (Universities Space Research Association / Ames Research Center), the WFC3 Science Oversight Committee, and the Hubble Heritage Team (STScI / AURA) (c); (bl). **8-9 NASA:** ESA, and The Hubble Heritage Team (STScI / AURA). **9 ESO:** (tr). **10 NASA:** WMAP Science Team (bl). **Science Photo Library:** Victor de Schwanberg (cl). **11 NASA:** Visible Earth (br). **Science Photo Library:** Chris Butler (tc). **12 NASA:** ESA, R.M. Crockett (University of Oxford, U.K.), S. Kaviraj (Imperial College London and University of Oxford, U.K.), J. Silk (University of Oxford), M. Mutchler (Space Telescope Science Institute, Baltimore, USA), R. O'Connell (University of Virginia, Charlottesville, USA), and the WFC3 Scientific Oversight Committee (c); ESA (bl). **12-13 NASA:** ESA and the Hubble Heritage (STScI / AURA)-ESA / Hubble Collaboration Acknowledgment: M. Crockett and S. Kaviraj (Oxford University, UK), R. O'Connell (University of Virginia), B. Whitmore (STScI) and the WFC3 Scientific Oversight Committee. **13 NASA:** ESA and the Hubble Heritage Team (STScI / AURA)-ESA / Hubble Collaboration. Acknowledgment: R. O'Connell (University of Virginia) and the WFC3 Scientific Oversight Committee (tl). **14 Corbis:** Matthew Russell / Visuals Unlimited (bc). **NASA:** ESA, and the Hubble Heritage Team (STScI / AURA). (cl). **14-15 NASA:** ESA, and the Hubble Heritage Team STScI / AURA)-ESA / Hubble Collaboration. **15 Max-Planck-Institut für Astrophysik:** (tr). **NASA:** ESA, the Hubble Heritage (STScI / AURA)-ESA / Hubble Collaboration, and A. Evans (University of Virginia, Charlottesville / NRAO / Stony Brook University) (cb). **16-17 Science Photo Library:** Chris Butler. **16 Science Photo Library:** Lynette Cook (bl). **17 The Art Archive:** National Gallery London / John Webb (br). **ESO:** B. Fugate (FASORtronics) (tc). **NASA:** X-ray: NASA / CXC / UMass / D. Wang et al.; Optical: NASA / ESA / STScI / D.Wang et al.; IR: NASA / JPL-Caltech / SSC / S.Stolovy (clb). **18-19 NASA:** JPL / Ames Research Center. **20 NASA:** Hinode JAXA / PPARC (cl). **Science Photo Library:** Scharmer et al, Royal Swedish Academy of Sciences (bl). **20-21 SOHO (ESA & NASA).** **21 Corbis:** NASA (cr); Jay Pasachoff (crb). **23 NASA:** ESA and M. Buie (cra/r); JPL / Ames Research Center (crb); JPL / DLR (cr); JPL-Caltech / University of Arizona (cra/l). **24-25 Corbis:** Roger Ressmeyer (Background). **NASA:** JPL / MSSS (c). **24 Mattias Malmer:** (cb). **NASA:** Johns Hopkins University Applied Physics Laboratory / Carnegie Institution of Washington (cl); JPL (crb/l); JPL-Caltech / ASU (bl, crb/r). **25 ESA:** DLR / FU Berlin (G. Neukum) (cb). **NASA:** Goddard Space Flight Center Scientific Visualization Studio (tc); JPL (cr). **26 NASA:** GFSC / Arizona State University (cl). **26-27 Corbis:** Roger Ressmeyer (Background). **NASA:** JPL / USGS (tc). **27 Michael Karrer:** (tr). **28-29 Corbis:** Roger Ressmeyer (Background). **28 NASA:** The Hubble Heritage Team (STScI / AURA) (br); JPL / University of Arizona (tl); JPL (cr). **29 Getty Images:** John Russell (cr). **NASA:** JPL (tr); Erich Karkoschka, University of Arizona (tl). **30 NASA:** JPL (cb, c). **31 Corbis:** Denis Scott (cra/r). **Japan Aerospace Exploration Agency (JAXA):** (tl). **NASA:** (cra/l); JPL / JHUAPL (c); JPL (bl); ESA, JPL, and A. Feild (STScI) (tr/r). **Science Photo Library:** Detlev van

Ravenswaay (br); Friedrich Saurer (tr/l, cr). **32-33 Science Photo Library:** Walter Pacholka, Astropics. **33 Corbis:** ALI JAREKJI (br). **NASA:** JPL / UMD (tl). **34-35 NASA:** ESA and the Hubble SM4 ERO Team. **36 Getty Images:** Library of Congress / digital version by Science Faction (tl); SSPL (tr). **36-37 Corbis:** Roger Ressmeyer (Background). **37 ESA:** NASA, ESA, H. Bond (STScI), and M. Barstow (University of Leicester) (bc). **Science Photo Library:** Jerry Lodriguss (ca). **38-39 ESO:** **38 NASA:** ESA, and J. Maĺz Apell·niz (Instituto de Astrofĺsica de Andalucĺa, Spain) (br); X-ray: NASA / CXC / U.Colorado / Linsky et al.; Optical: NASA / ESA / STScI / ASU / J. Hester & P.Scowen (bl). **40 NASA:** ESA, P. Kalas, J. Graham, E. Chiang, E. Kite (University of California, Berkeley), M. Clampin (NASA Goddard Space Flight Center), M. Fitzgerald (Lawrence Livermore National Laboratory), and K. Stapelfeldt and J. Krist (NASA Jet Propulsion Laboratory) (cra); (bl). **40-41 Science Photo Library:** Detlev van Ravenswaay. **41 NASA:** NOAA (tr). **Science Photo Library:** Dr Seth Shostak (cr). **42 ESA:** Hubble (bl). **42-43 ESA:** Hubble. **43 ESO:** (bl). **44-45 Corbis:** Roger Ressmeyer. **46 Corbis:** Roger Ressmeyer (bc). **Science Photo Library:** David Nunuk (cb). **46-47 Corbis:** Roger Ressmeyer. **47 ESO:** G. Huedepohl (tl); Swinburne Astronomy Productions (cr). **Science Photo Library:** Dr Juerg Alean (br). **48 NASA:** ESA / JHU / R.Sankrit & W.Blair (cl). **48-49 NASA.** **49 ESA:** AOES Medialab; background: Hubble Space Telescope image (NASA / ESA / STScI) (tc). **Getty Images:** Kim Westerskov (cra/Background). **NASA:** CXC / NGST (tr); (tl). **50-51 Corbis:** Sergei Ilnitsky / epa. **50 Getty Images:** McClatchy-Tribune (br). **51 Getty Images:** NASA (tr). **52 NASA:** Johns Hopkins University Applied Physics Laboratory / Carnegie Institution of Washington (cl); Johns Hopkins University Applied Physics Laboratory / Southwest Research Institute (bc). **52-53 NASA:** JPL. **53 ESA:** C.Carreau (tl). **NASA:** JPL (bc); JSC (ca). **54 Science Photo Library:** Detlev van Ravenswaay (cl). **54-55 NASA:** JPL / Cornell University. **55 ESA:** (br). **Getty Images:** Gamma-Keystone (cla). **NASA:** JPL-Caltech (cra). **56-57 Moonpans.com:** Mike Constantine. **58 Alamy Images:** ITAR-TASS Photo Agency (bl). **Corbis:** Brooks Kraft / Sygma (bc/r). **NASA:** (br); (cla). **Science Photo Library:** Ria Novosti (bc/l). **58-59 NASA:** JAXA. **59 NASA:** (cra). **Science Photo Library:** NASA (tl, br); Ria Novosti (crb). **60-61 NASA:** (Background); (c). **60 NASA:** (crb); (cl). **61 NASA:** (cla); (tr, br). **62 NASA:** (cla). **62-63 NASA:** ESA, and J. Garvin (NASA / GSFC). **63 NASA:** (tl, clb, crb). **64 NASA:** (c). **64-65 NASA.** **65 Corbis:** Ocean (tc/r); Roger Ressmeyer (tl). **NASA:** (tc/l, cr, br). **66-67 NASA.** **66 NASA:** (clb, br). **67 NASA:** (tr, cra, br). **69 NASA:** Johns Hopkins University Applied Physics Laboratory / Carnegie Institution of Washington (br). **70-71 NASA:** JPL. **72 NASA:** The Hubble Heritage Team (STScI / AURA) (br)

**Jacket images:** *Front:* **NASA:** ESA, A. Nota (ESA / STScI) (Background); **Science Photo Library:** David Ducros ca; *Back:* **Getty Images:** Thomas Collins cla; **iStockphoto.com:** Mischa Gossen c; **NASA:** ESA, A. Nota (ESA / STScI) (Background), JPL / Cornell University (Mars Rover) br

All other images © Dorling Kindersley
For further information see:
**www.dkimages.com**